THE SONG STARS

THE LADIES WHO SANG WITH THE BANDS AND BEYOND

by

RICHARD GRUDENS

Author of *The Best Damn Trumpet Player*

CELEBRITY PROFILES PUBLISHING
Stony Brook, New York 11790-0344

CANDID PHOTOS BY
C. CAMILLE SMITH AND GUS YOUNG

Library of Congress
Catalog Card Number 97-66866

ISBN 1-57579-045-9

Published by:
Celebrity Profiles Publishing Inc.
Box 344, Main Street
Stony Brook, New York 11790-0344
(516) 862-8555
Fax (516) 862-0139
E-Mail Rickgru@AOL.COM

Edited by MaryLou Facciola

Printed in United States of America

PINE HILL PRESS, INC.
Freeman, S. Dak. 57029

ACKNOWLEDGMENTS

I wish to express my sincere gratitude to the following:

Frankie Laine, one of show business' most beloved personalities, for his encouragement and his dedication to the music we all love. Above all, he loves to sing.

Connie Haines for her enthusiasm and all-around help and ideas.

Jack Ellsworth for his ongoing assistance and cornucopia of knowledge which he shared so generously.

Don Kennedy for his consistent commitment to preserving the memory of all the participants of the Big Band Era and beyond.

Camille Smith and Gus Young for their sensitive photographs.

Joe Graydon for his assistance with Helen Forrest.

Jo Stafford for her soft voice, good editing, and great photo.

Kitty Kallen for her personal all-around help and encouragement.

Warren Covington, my friend, pen pal, and supporter.

Bill Munroe for his assistance with Teresa Brewer.

Alan Eichler for his assistance with Anita O'Day.

Al "Jazzbeaux Collins" for being "Jazzbeaux."

Red Norvo for his assistance with Mildred Bailey.

Lee Hale and Ray Charles (the other) for their willing assistance.

Mike Prelee for sharing his wealth of knowledge and information.

Jack Rael for help and insight into his lifetime protégé Patti Page.

André Doudot for his help with Josephine Baker.

WQEW's Jonathan Schwartz and Bob Jones for keeping the music going.

The folks at Pine Hill Press for all they do so well.

My wife, Jeanette, for giving up much of her time allowing me to fulfill my need to produce this book.

My son, Peter, for introducing me to the Computer Age which enabled me to put this chronicle together.

My editor, Mary Lou Facciola, for her patient efforts, good suggestions, and valuable advice.

Last, but not least, all the singers themselves.

TABLE OF CONTENTS

PART THREE:

FOREWORD

by Connie Haines

Life is one big adventure. As a teenager, I got my start during the Big Band Era being discovered by Harry James. My name was Yvonne Marie Antoinette Ja Mais. Considering this, Harry said, "What are we going to do with that on a marquee'? There sure would be no room for me. You look like a 'Connie'—Connie Haines that blends with James." Well that was my beginning, a lot like the start of many a youngster who found themselves singing in what would become The Big Band Era. For example, Doris Day was Doris Kappelhoff. Lynn Roberts was Leonore Raisig, Helen Forrest was Helen Fogel and Dolly Dawn was Teresa Stabile.

I was lucky. I found myself singing with a young fellow named Frank Sinatra and backed up by Jo Stafford and the Pied Pipers in an organization led by the wonderful Tommy Dorsey where we produced all those wonderful recordings that you have in your collections. The songs we sang then are the same I sing at concerts today. That musical era featured a lions share of great musicians, talented arrangers, and those wonderful men and ladies who sang with those bands in their own unique style. It surely can never be duplicated again. We know that now.

Today, the "estate bands" fill the ever-demanding market even though they are led by different leaders, usually alumni of the earlier versions of those bands. Some call them "ghost bands." They still tour the country, packing them in at every Performing Arts Center and College auditorium and at places like Las Vegas and Atlantic City. What a heritage! The boy and girl singers (that's what they called us in those days) are known today simply as Song Stars.

My 1996 California tour with Larry Elgart's band was sold out in packed auditoriums everywhere we traveled. We were thrilled and amazed. The same story exists for Rosemary Clooney, maybe in Atlantic City or New York City at a club here or there. It also applies to Big Band singers Kay Starr, Anita O'Day, Fran Warren, Peggy Lee, Helen Forrest, Bea Wain, The King Sisters, Kitty Kallen, Martha Tilton and Doris Day when they do and if they do. It's amazing that after all these many years the public still adores their song singing heroes of past generations. We must have been pretty good. That, of course, goes for all the boys too. We'll hear about them in a forthcoming subsequent book.

We have recently lost many of our lady Song Stars, but they will never be forgotten. Among them, Ella Fitzgerald who sang with Chick Webb, Helen O'Connell of Jimmy Dorsey's band, Paula Kelly and Marion Hutton of Glenn Miller's group, June Christie who sang with Stan Kenton, and Carmen McCrae.

As one of those Song Stars, I have been privileged to entertain American audiences from one end of the United States to the other throughout the years. For me and the others it was an exciting and rewarding experience as we traversed from one city to another passing one another like ships in the night to bring what I call True American Music to our fans. What an honor it has been to sing for you all my life.

Now, read on. This book will tell you the story, however short, of each of these Song Stars, including my own. My friend Richard Grudens has brought it all back to life in this memorable book and I have written this opening page to get you started.

See you later, I'm on my way to sing a Big Band concert now.

Connie Haines, Clearwater Beach, Florida
February 5, 1997

PREFACE

Soon after the publication of *The Best Damn Trumpet Player* in 1996, I received a spirited letter from Connie Haines. Connie, of course, is the quintessential band vocalist. She was absolutely insulted that a chapter chronicling her colorful career was not included in the book. Responding to a "Comments Form" about the book enclosed in a mailing that reached Connie at her Florida home, she bellowed:

"Why didn't you interview me?"

Well, the girl was right. Her story surely belonged between those covers. But, a number of performers were not profiled within the modest 200 page chronicle. Simultaneously, and coincidentally, Pied Piper leader (also a Florida resident), bandleader and trombonist Warren Covington thought it a good idea to create a sequel to *The Best Damn Trumpet Player* covering the careers of, as Tony Bennett once described to me, "all those other talented guys and ladies who sing and play the great classic music of our time."

So the spark was kindled by Tommy Dorsey's favorite trombonist Warren Covington and girl singer Connie Haines. Hence this book. When I queried some booksellers of current and out-of print jazz and music books, Arthur L. Newman of Newman's Bookstore of Fountain Valley, California, simply said: "The new book sounds great. I am sure it will do very well. It has not been done before and will be in demand. I'll start with an order for 100 copies when it's ready." That did it!

My earliest interest in all Song Stars began on March 15, 1952. I was a NBC volunteer working on Jerry Lewis and Dean Martin's very first telethon, being the person who admitted the talent, documenting the length of time each participant appeared on camera. Just review this extraordinary list of Song Stars, male and female, who passed through my gate that single day : Vivian Blaine, Rosemarie, Frances Langford, Ezio Pinza, Yul Brynner, Nat "King" Cole, Martha

Wright, Dean Martin, Perry Como, Juanita Hall, Cab Calloway, Sarah Vaughan, Harry Belafonte, Celeste Holm, Ella Fitzgerald, Connee Boswell, Frank Sinatra, Helen O'Connell, the DeMarco Sisters, Kay Arman, and then Private Eddie Fisher. I was nineteen and smitten for sure by the likes of these Song Stars.

Over the years, many words have been printed elsewhere about the participants of the Big Band Era and beyond, but never at one time or in one single book, at least for many years. Some subjects have had books written about them, and some have penned their autobiography. Most of these, however, are more personal and emotional, even despairing stories rather than presentations of pure musical adventure.

Rosemary Clooney delivered *This Is Remembrance*, an account of a shattered life that eventually emerged happy and fulfilling for this accomplished Irish-American singer. Connie Haines book, *For Once in My Life,* details her compelling, inspiring success story in 225 interesting and sometimes uplifting spiritual pages of a life that began in childhood and concluded in the Seventies when the book went to press. Helen Forrest's 1982 *I Had the Craziest Dream* autobiography was very sentimental and details special periods of her life. Early innovator Bessie Smith's *Bessie: Empress of the Blues* by Chris Albertson is a riveting, melodramatic, and detailed biography of her life and times.

We all know the tragedy that was Billie Holiday. The book *Billie's Blues* by John Chilton was a good biography of one of the completely original giants of jazz, and the autobiography *Lady Sings the Blues* with William Dufty is a roughened tear-jerker that was turned into a poor film facsimile, no disrespect to the wonderful Diana Ross, another song star who played Billie in that movie. *Wishing on the Moon*, another Billie Holiday book by Donald Clarke, was more sociological than musical.

Doris Day's entry *Her Own Story*, an autobiography written with A.E. Hotchner, was also better than most such books. It's an organized chronicle with other voices as vignettes located at strategic points, but otherwise mostly a personal, candid look at her charming and sometimes trying life. The Ella Fitzgerald book, *A Biography of the First Lady of Jazz*, is a book of mostly second hand information, mostly because Ella was never available for interviews (at that particular time), so the book is mostly musical and contains a great discography.

Respected writer and music producer Gene Lees has documented uncounted pages about some of the subjects represented in this book and *The Best Damn Trumpet Player,* among others, as has Will Friedwald in his various books, especially *Jazz Singing.* Lees' intimate, indepth accounts of the careers of Jo Stafford, Peggy Lee, Edith Piaf, Sarah Vaughan, and others of note are considered more serious and analytical. Lees worked, traveled and sometimes lived among his subjects, permitting him exceptional, sensitive access to very important figures of the Jazz Age. His books are excellent and not to be missed, if this *genre'* piques your interest. Will Friedwald has presented much historical information mixed with strong, sometimes controversial opinion. Nevertheless, it's a must read too.

However, a consideration known as the aging process has set many of the surviving vocalists, who were members of one band or another, well aside the limelight, if not in complete retirement, with the exception of a few who today are still able to dazzle an audience. But, time marches on, so the saying goes, and the body of work accomplished by most of these vocalists rests within the recordings we have wisely preserved.

The collection of words about that music contained between these covers is more loosely drawn and more lightly presented, covering less intensive detail, but illustrating for its readers more anecdotal and uplifting reports about their favorite vocalists and the songs that represented their presence to several, past generations of music lovers. As Buddy Rich once told me, "This is not a step back, this is not nostalgia, this is music to my ears."

Poignantly enough, this portion of the book's *introduction* is being composed on the afternoon of June 15, 1996, the day the life of the First Lady of Song, Ella Fitzgerald, sadly passed away from us. So, as buoyant as this book intends to be, the passing of Ella punctuates the humanity of all its participants. They are more than larger-than-life celebrities; they are vulnerable human beings as well, like the rest of us. Although Ella stood larger than life, her outgoing, personal warmth fused our connection to her and the others as not just voices on a radio or images on a television screen, but as authentic human beings—maybe wives, mothers, and grandmothers—who sing but also live and love.

These warm-hearted chapters about the singers and their music are written exclusively to be celebrated and enjoyed. They are meant to evoke memories of those remarkable performers you love. They will take you home for a moment once again to a more reasonable, simpler and probably a more enjoyable time of your life, when music made sense and you could sing or whistle along, dance or simply lie back and listen to your favorite vocalist.

Richard Grudens, Stony Brook, NY
February, 1997

Working together in April 1989. L to R (top row): Phyllis, Christine and Dorothy McGuire; (bottom row): Teresa Brewer, Margaret Whiting, Patti Page, Fran Warren. (Bill Munroe Collection)

THE LADIES WHO SANG WITH THE BANDS

Words and Music by Lee Hale

There were Big Bands and small bands and combos and such;
Back in the forties, we loved them so much
There were sections of brass and reeds and rhythm,
And one more ingredient that always went with 'em

******

In front of the band facing swingers and squares,
The Ladies Who Sang With The Bands,
Sitting all night on those hard folding chairs,
The Ladies Who Sang With The Bands
They went on the road playing ballrooms and dives,
Going through hell with those orchestra wives;
But how they could floor us, with one little chorus:
The Ladies Who Sang With The Bands.

Their records made hist'ry and money galore;
And oh, those recordings were grand;
But somehow there weren't any royalties for
The Ladies Who Sang With The Bands.
Sitting and Smiling, they'd wait to go on;
Wondering when they could go to the john.
Regrets they had none of,
I wish I'd been one of
The Ladies Who Sang With, just one of the gang with,
The Ladies Who Sang With The Bands

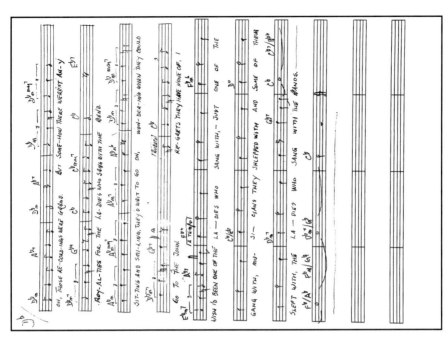

Author Lee Hale's original "Lead" sheet sketched out for the Arranger Jon Charles. (Ray Charles collection)

**Frankie Laine and Richard Grudens talk about Edith Piaf.
(Photo C. Camille Smith)**

SOME SINGERS I HAVE KNOWN

by Frankie Laine

Rich Grudens has invited me to share my impressions of the lady singers I have known and worked with over the more than 40 years in the singing business. It's a pleasure to search back through my memory bank and reminisce about these talented and successful women who so strongly influenced the music of our time.

I will begin with an unusual singer, Edith Piaf, who was sort of special to me. When I first heard about her, I was in New York and she was appearing at the Blue Angel. I had never heard her before so I decided to go and see her act. I loved her version of *La Vie en rose* which she sung that night. Apparently somebody told her I was in the house and she surprised me by announcing my presence. I was very flattered and took a bow. Then she sent word from backstage that she'd like to meet me after the show. We met and talked for a long time. I was very entranced with Edith Piaf. She was known the world over as the "Little Sparrow;" I guess because she was a tiny person. She was a real *pixie gamin*—that's a French expression that characterizes a sort of homeless girl who roams about the streets.

I loved the uniqueness of her sounds—you know, the way she interprets a song—that's the only way I can describe it. It wasn't a great voice, but a voice from a small body that you would call a sort of stylish dishing up what she felt the song demanded of her. I've always said you do the best you can with what you've got. She did better than that. She did a lot more than was demanded of her. On stage she was absolutely charming. Offstage she was very natural. You would never think she was a great star. She never talked show business talk.

Anyway, I put that meeting behind me for a while until I went to Paris in 1957 to perform for 10 weeks at a place called the Olympia.

1

I was recording the first foreign album with conductor Michel LeGrand. Edith heard I was in town. She called me and later threw a big bash party at the close of my engagement. It was one of the best times in Nan's and my life. We went to her place and sat around and had what you can only call a giant barbecue. It was just wonderful, and she was a gracious hostess, and Nan and I were absolutely honored to be her guests.

She encouraged Charles Aznavour, Edith's songwriter and singer in his own right, and me to go around to different "courtyards" of house clusters. Being French, Charles was able to gain entrance. So as sort of a PR gag, he would shout that he and Frankie Laine were here to serenade the people. Then we would sing, and they would actually throw money at us. I had such a wonderful and amazing time during the period of my friendship with Edith Piaf and her friends.

Now I would like to mention some associations with other Song Stars I have known. First, I must tell you about lovely Jo Stafford. She and I go back a long way, and she is probably one of the greatest voices I have ever worked with, and that's why I have included all her duets that we recorded together on some recent CD's. Jo Stafford has perfect pitch. It's truly amazing to listen to her sing. When you listen carefully, even though you may not know a lot about music, you cannot escape that fact.

Peggy Lee invited me to sing on her *Chesterfield Supper Club* show many times. Not too long ago, Peg and I did a tribute to Jim Conklin, the guy who started Capitol Records with Glen Wallach and who also started Warner Brothers Records. Peg was one of his star singers. Peg is great. She will do things like that to show her appreciation. You know, one of the best records she ever made was a song called *Mr. Wonderful*. It is an underrated performance and much overlooked. It's one of the best things I ever heard from any singer.

Connie Haines and I are old friends for sure. I recently sent her a long letter just to renew our long-lasting friendship. We once did a TV show together called *Partners*. We also toured together for a while. The date I remember most was in Providence, Rhode Island, when I first started touring. She was simply wonderful and a worthy singer and I always felt comfortable working with her.

Marie Ellington, who was Nat Cole's wife, is a good singer and a very special friend. I hadn't talked to her for a long time—I had lost her number—and Richard Grudens was able to obtain her address. For years I was trying to find her. She had sent Richard an endorsement of his book, *The Best Damn Trumpet Player*, and she had asked about me. So I contacted her and we talked quite a bit. I first knew her when she married Nat "King" Cole. I was so close to Nat at that time. When Nat passed on, Marie gave me one of his money clips for a remembrance. When Nat had his TV show and many performers wouldn't appear on his show because he was black, I did it and she never could appreciate it enough. But I did it because I admired Nat "King" Cole and he was an influence in my singing career. I was proud and glad to be his friend and would do anything to help him. Marie sang with Duke Ellington and did a great job. Ellington said she was one of his best singers. She is also the mother of Natalie Cole, a credit to her father I might add.

I never worked with Lena Horne, but she recorded a CD entitled *We'll Be Together Again,* which I much appreciated. We got to know one another at MGM when I worked under her future husband, Lennie Hayton. I was in the MGM choir, when I was just beginning. We are still friends.

Doris Day is one of the best singers this country has ever known. I got to know her when we recorded a terrific song called *Sugarbush*. I have always loved Doris, and I like what she does today helping all those helpless animals. This proves what kind of a person I always knew she was.

Anita O'Day and I go back to the early Marathon dancing days. She was just 14 years old and used to follow me around asking me a million questions in her quest to learn the singing business. She would ask me about phrasing and why I sang this way or that way. She followed me around like a puppy. When they found out she was but 14, they pulled her out of the Marathons. But it was quite a learning experience for her. Once, when she got a job in a club, she tried to get me in too. She was an excellent singer. Time has proven all that.

Patti Page and I worked together quite a bit over the years. We took her into the Paramount in New York and the Chicago Theater in 1950. She was new then. Later, in 1952, we toured with Billy May. It was her first tour. Then we once did a series of shows on Long Island (Westbury Music Fair) and also in Massachusetts. We have been very close over the years. Her longtime manager, Jack Rael, and I have been friends for many years too.

With Rosemary Clooney, I did a Thirtieth Anniversary show for *The Dick Clark Show* at the Waldorf Astoria in New York in 1991. All the old gang was there from the early recording days: Mitch Miller, Guy Mitchell, The Four Lads, and other Miller protégés. It was a great show. Rosemary is still a stunning performer.

Over the years I have worked with many, many lady singers. It was I who introduced Helen O'Connell to Jimmy Dorsey. I've worked with Keely Smith, and I remember watching the great Billie Holiday, who was also an influence on my career as was Mildred Bailey, another one of the great early singers. She enthralled me very early on the song *Rocking Chair*, one of her hits, because I like the way she did it. I still maintain a friendship today with Mildred's husband Red Norvo in whose orchestra she sang.

Although I have never worked with Helen Forrest, I consider her the best singer Artie Shaw ever had and one of the fine singers of the era. My friendship with her through the Society of Singers continues today. I've always admired Teresa Brewer too; her husband Bob Thiele was one of my first producers at ABC Records. I've never worked with Kitty Kallen either, but we are friends and hope to get together soon. She is also one of the best singers I have ever heard, as is Dinah Shore, Frances Langford, and Bea Wain, too. There are just so many good singers to remember.

I could go on forever about the wonderful Song Stars who appear in this book, but I think their stories in this book speak for all of them. Read on, enjoy, and thanks.

Frankie Laine, San Diego, California
March, 1997

Jack Ellsworth, General Manager of WLIM Radio in New York and
Song Star expert. (Photo C. Camille Smith)

THOSE WONDERFUL GIRL SINGERS

by Jack Ellsworth

The writers and reviewers of the popular music magazines *Swing, Orchestra World*, *Metronome* and *Downbeat* called them canaries, chirps, thrushes or warblers back in the Big Band days. They were the girl singers of the Big Bands who decorated the bandstand and delighted fans in theaters, hotels, and dance halls. Probably the most successful vocalists who started with those bands, then eventually achieved success on their own, were Doris Day (Les Brown), Peggy Lee (Benny Goodman), Ella Fitzgerald (Chick Webb), Rosemary Clooney (Tony Pastor), Jo Stafford (Tommy Dorsey), June Christy (Stan Kenton), and Anita O'Day (Gene Krupa), who uses her voice like a musical instrument.

They were the exceptions. The majority of girl singers were known mostly by their Big Band association and were usually introduced with "formerly featured with" notations, for example: Helen Ward and Martha Tilton with Benny Goodman, and Helen Forrest (often called the ultimate or definitive big band vocalist) with Shaw, Goodman and James. Connie Haines, Helen O'Connell, and Kitty Kallen also fall into that category, but in time became more well-known personalities than the latter group.

There were many female vocalists who had limited and less memorable associations with various bands of the era: Marion Hutton (Glenn Miller), Bea Wain (Larry Clinton), Bonnie Baker (Orrin Tucker), Ginny Sims and Georgia Carroll (Kay Kyser), Francis Wayne (Woody Herman), and Fran Warren (Claude Thornhill), a cut above most band singers achieving many Broadway road shows successes, as well.

6

Georgia Carroll and Kay Kyser. (Richard Grudens Collection)

Forgive me if I have omitted the likes of Dolly Dawn, Dorothy Collins and Betty Hutton. They were more personality types than singers. I don't remember much about Bob Chester's Dodie O'Neill and Ozzie Nelson's Harriet Hilliard, although they certainly pleased the crowds. Ozzie and Harriet, of course, became man and wife and enjoyed many successful seasons on radio and television in shows bearing their names.

I think you'll agree that no indelible connection existed between Kay Starr and bandleaders Joe Venuti, Charlie Barnet, and Glenn Miller; and who really recalls Lena Horne singing with Charlie Barnet or Noble Sissle. Sarah Vaughan began with Earl Hines all right, and Billie Holiday did sing briefly with both Basie and Artie Shaw, but they achieved success mostly without Big Band assistance.

In 1950 I attended a Billie Holiday show at the Famous Door nightclub on New York's 52nd Street. I can picture her now, tall and lovely in a blue gown with the signature white carnation nestled in her hair. With that great charisma and powerful, emotional delivery, she has undoubtedly influenced hundreds of girl singers who have followed in her footsteps.

Tommy Tucker's Amy Arnell, Johnny Long's Helen Young, Teddy Powell's Ruth Gaylor, and Dorothy Claire with Bobby Byrne and Glenn Miller were likable vocalists but depended more on their looks than musical talent. Lynn Roberts, Paula Kelly, June Hutton, and Jo Ann Greer had brief associations with bands as did many, many others—too many to mention here.

Pretty Lucy Ann Polk sang with Tommy Dorsey in the late forties and did a fine solo album in 1957. Jo Ann Greer was a mainstay with Les Brown. Her heartfelt rendition of *Where Are You* is really something. Seventeen year old Lynn Roberts also sang with Dorsey in 1950. A friend, she still performs today. Some say that Harry James declared, "She is the best girl singer I ever had." Her MGM album, *Harry, You Made Me Love You*, was recorded in 1983 as a tribute to James and is class from the very first groove.

Here is my list of five all-time favorite female singers in no particular order:

Ella Fitzgerald—The First Lady of Song for over half a century.

Sarah Vaughan—The most glorious voice ever.

Carmen McRae—An astonishing talent.

Rosemary Clooney—A unique sound-smooth, sexy and still swingin'!

Teddi King—a darling girl, who left us while still in her prime. She had so much to offer. *Metronome* magazine once called her "a nearly perfect singer."

I must add honorable mentions to both classy Doris Day and swinging June Christy.

The very first female vocalist to impress me was Helen Rowland with the Fred Rich Orchestra. She sang *I'm Yours* on an early Thirties, fifteen-cent cardboard *Hit of the Week* recording. I was but ten and dug her sound even then. I also enjoyed radio's Annette Hanshaw, and Frances Langford with Dick Powell on *Hollywood Hotel* broadcasts. Ruth Etting also had a distinctive quality. Anyone remember Edna O'Dell on those early WJZ *Breakfast Club* broadcasts?

Then there is Helen Ward and liltin' Martha Tilton-both with Benny Goodman. Over the years I think Benny featured more girl singers—however briefly—than any other leader. There was Ella Fitzgerald (Yes, even Ella), Frances Hunt, Frances Langford, Monica Lewis, "the singing rage" Miss Patti Page, Rosemary Clooney (including a rare '50's recording), Louise Tobin, Anita O'Day, Mildred Bailey, Sandy Stewart, Carrie Smith, and over 40 more. This was, of course, over a period of 50 years.

There was Mindy Carson, Nan Wynn, Barbara McNair, Joannie Somers, and Toni Harper, who all surfaced briefly—then were gone. Lurlean Hunter came from Chicago with a smooth, sultry voice. Her four 1950's albums are now considered collectors' treasures.

How about Judy Garland? Her 1961 Carnegie Hall concert album still gives me goose bumps. She was in a class by herself. Not a band singer, except in the movies.

9

Great music also flowed from the hearts of Maxine Sullivan, Dinah Washington, Margaret Whiting, Keely Smith, Kay Starr, Jerri Southern, and Georgia Brown-wonderful vocalists all.

Dinah Shore was always a consistent performer. Eydie Gorme is still going strong. *If He Walked Into My Life Today* thrills every time. And there's marvelous Marlene ver Plank. No one sings better. Carol Sloane's jazz CD's are great, and Barbra Streisand is a true superstar, but becomes overly dramatic as does Diane Schuur and Nancy Wilson.

Vicki Carr, Gogi Grant, Julie London, Della Reese, Eileen Farrell, Morgana King, Leslie Uggams, Diahann Carroll, Lee Wiley, Connee Boswell, and the clear sound of Felicia Sanders are always great expressions.

Oh, there are so many, many good singers. Old favorite Beryl Davis, sweet Betty Johnson, Jackie Cain (with or without Roy Kral). And what about Toni Arden and Sue Raney—both very talented. Susannah McCorkle and Ernestine Anderson's recordings are swell, too. The voice of Karen Carpenter cannot be overstated. Her Christmas collection is really magnificent. I loved those low notes.

Toni Tennille—fine without the Captain; Natalie Cole—when she sings smooth songs, Sue Mathews and Nancy La Mott, Mabel Mercer and Sylvia Sims. All part of the "who's who" destined for the female vocalists history charts.

I remember a Connie Haines interview in 1950 where I told her how much I admired her recording *Snootie Little Cutie* made with Frank Sinatra and Tommy Dorsey. Connie said that Frank would tease her a lot in those early days:

"I tried to stay away from him. In the studio they had me on one mike and Frank on another each at opposite sides of the studio. And here we are singing all these cute little bits to each other while I was glaring at him. But that didn't last long...we eventually became friends."

So start turning pages and read on about some of these worthy favorites. If I have left someone out, please forgive me. We really loved to hear them all. As Buddy Rich once stated about the players and singers of the Big Band Era and beyond, "You can't insult all the other giants, so all of them are my favorites." We have to agree with Buddy.

Stay tuned.

Jack Ellsworth, President and General Manager
of Radio Station WLIM
Patchogue, New York November, 1996

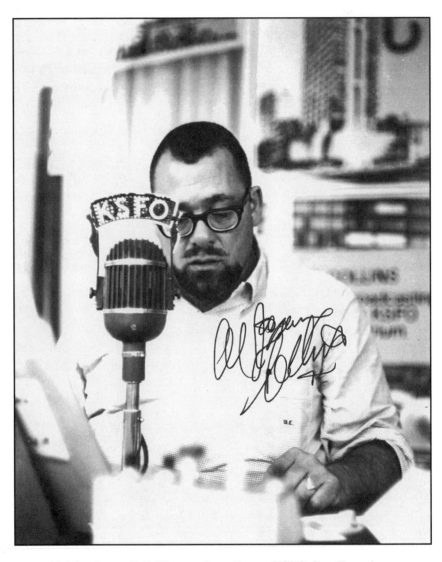

Al "Jazzbeaux" Collins at the mike on KSFO San Francisco.

LIFE IN THE PURPLE GROTTO

by Al "Jazzbeaux" Collins

"Hi! My name is Jazzbeaux. And I want to tell you about a disc jockey that I know from Salt Lake City, who really knows his business. He knows jazz, he knows music, and he does stunts on the air that will bring credit to your station. And he's not your ordinary disc jockey......."

Well, the above text was pretty much the words I used during an impromptu, spur-of-the-moment audition for a job at a New York radio station called WNEW. The station's general manager, Miss Bernice Judis, a kind of brilliant, dedicated administrator (some say she liked radios the way some men liked cars), admired the sound of my voice. After those first words the engineer interrupted me from the control room and said: "Miss Judis would like you to put a couple of records together and make up a little program."

So I went into the record library and got some Mel Torme', some Count Basie, and some Lena Horne...Shearing too. I introduced these records and I used music behind me as I was talking. To my knowledge that's the first time that any jockey used that device. And it sounded like I was coming out of a club or something. It relaxed me because I could think between sentences, and there wouldn't be a pause that would be awkward. At first she said *no*, but after talking awhile about Basie and the others, the engineer interrupted and said, "Well, she wants to see you." So I went into her office and up the thick diamond-shaped carpet and the great-lookin' furniture and she hired me.

Before that I was a pretty successful jock on KDIL in Salt Lake City. I grew a beard during that period for something called Pioneer Day and just kept it. Bernice thought it was kinda weird, so I told her I would shave it off.

13

"I wouldn't give a damn if your entire body and face were covered with hair" she said, "do you talk like that all the time?" I said, 'Yeah, I do'. Then she said, "Can you start Thursday?"

Well, I had to give notice to my job in Salt Lake City. So I did and the manager there, Sid Fox, gave me the green light. "Go. Jazzbeaux, take your opportunity and go, with my blessing." So I did.

The first night I went to work, I was assigned to Studio 1, and the entire studio was purple. I got on the air at 9:35, and earlier the engineer said I should use the word jazz in my title and the only word we could think of was *jazzbeaux* which was kind of an old invention—a pre-tied, elastic bow-tie already made up that you could slip around your neck in a second, so I said, "This is Jazzbeaux and I'm in the Purple Grotto." And I had my Nat Cole going underneath it, the piano music, and I said, "Yeah, you know, I play jazz music, but you can't play jazz in a fluorescently lit air-conditioned studio, it's too clinical, there's just no atmosphere, so I came down here this afternoon, it's beneath the studios and it's really beautiful. It's a Grotto. A Purple Grotto."

And that's how I got started in big time New York. I created an imaginary world in the minds of my listeners, just as Martin Block did with his Make Believe Ballroom. Soon I was sending out solid purple specially photographed postcards with the bold caption: Al "Jazzbeaux" Collins at work in the Purple Grotto.

I had fun in the Grotto. I discovered little animals and things that lived down there...and..I used to enlarge on those. It kept the show fresh, and...kept the imagination going and fired. I had an owl down there which is still on my show today. His name was Harrison and he was named after Harrison Kinne of the *New Yorker* magazine. He was in the Grotto one night and out of the blue he says, "Hey, Jazzbeaux, what are those two orange lights back there?" Of course I went along and said, "That's Harrison, my owl." I didn't call him Harrison before that. Then I said, "That's my owl, a long-tailed, purple Tasmanian owl," which sounded very descriptive to me.

In those days I did a live show out of the Embers night club where they had different piano players every night. A half hour, we'd have Teddy Wilson, we'd have Art Tatum, Marian McPartland, a whole bunch of other people. Harrison and I would get on the subway (that's what I told the listeners). But, just before that I would put on a six minute record and, by the time it started, I was downstairs in a waiting taxicab on my way to the Embers. By the time the music ended, it sounded like I opened a door, and there I was in the night club, at the Embers. That transition really worked. A lot of people believed it. Actually WNEW was on Forty-sixth and Fifth avenue and the Embers up on Third Avenue, close by. I made people think I was taking the subway with Harrison...like on a special train that I used to get on.

When Art Ford left WNEW I finally ended up with that all night show, over there at the "Milkman's Matinee." I worked it from midnight till five in the morning. A tough time but it never bothered me. My idea was that you worked your job and that's what you're supposed to be doing. I was happy being on the air. I was on the outstanding radio station in the country that broadcasted to about eight different provinces and states in New York at the same time. It was 50,000 watts, just like NBC.

After six years at WNEW I left a few times but always came back. One time is when I worked at NBC for a while from four in the afternoon and then 9:35 till eleven at night for a few years inbetween. But I didn't even mind that. Even though I came from Brooklyn, New York, I thought of Salt Lake City as my comfortable home. The second time back at WNEW I picked up my old shows just like before. But I insisted on playing jazz, an unheard of thing at the time. I wouldn't play any fad music or things like *Mairzy Doats* and all those novelty tunes. They gave me license to pick my own stuff and manage my own program. So they got my jazz and got used to hearing George Shearing, Mel Torme', Anita O'Day, Dinah Washington, some Peggy Lee, and Ella-mostly Ella-and all those people who were in the upper echelon of good music.

Jazz artists would show up. Count Basie surprised me one morning by coming up. Freddie Green, his guitar player came in, and Thad Jones and a few of the other guys came up too. We'd end up with a whole orchestra in the studio. Some days I would throw all the commercials out the window, and had just a hell of a show. The drive from Basie's band appealed to me, so I played a lot of Basie. I guess I had a lot of power in those days.

15

After about ten or eleven years I wanted to go out to San Francisco 'cause I heard it was great out there. So I called a couple of stations and I said, "My name in Al Collins and I want to work in San Francisco." One station manager says to me, "Al Collins? Are you Jazzbeaux?" I didn't know anybody knew me outside of New York. So I said, "Yes, I am." Then he says, "Well, hell! You should come out and let us hear you. I'll send you a ticket," and he did.

I got on the plane and went to the station, KSFO, and got on the air and did a live audition. I did a show I called "Collins on the Cloud" (like I did in Manhattan) and I was able to float over San Francisco and I was able to see the things you would see from the air—like Alcatraz and the bridge-all done with harp music behind me. That gave the thing an ethereal feeling and people were wondering what was going on. They loved it. The show clicked and I got a spread in *Newsweek* and *Fortune* magazines. Harrison came with me to Frisco and I still went to the Embers and he would make screams and sounds from his spot on top of the handlebars of the cart we were traveling in. One night he screamed so loud that it caused an avalanche and the tunnel caved in and I had to get him oxygen. So I asked people to send me drinking straws and I would poke them through and give him some air....and you should have seen the straws that came into the station. It was unbelievable.

Calls would come in and they'd want to know if he was doing ok...if he was still breathing. All that stuff added some realism to my programs. Sure, it was great calling out artists and tunes, but I didn't care exclusively about that. I wanted some story line behind what I was doing. The Grotto still exists today. It's on wheels and I can take it home with me or to any other station. It's like play to me.

I've lost lots of jobs earlier because I wouldn't do the standard thing, like write spots or do this or that that a manager wanted. I am different and always do my own thing. I was interested in new ideas all the time. There was that need, and as long as I could get away with it, I was free and able to do what I wanted to do.

I always wanted to do a national network jazz show. The closest I got was when I did the *Tonite Show* at the end of Steve Allen's rein. It was only for a few weeks but I had Jack Teagarden and Erroll Garner and others on. I've done all kinds of crazy disc jockey stuff like in Salt Lake City when I broadcasted from "under the Great Salt Lake," and the time in 1950 I played Art Mooney's recording of *I'm Looking Over a Four Leaf Clover* over 50 times in one day, one play right after another, although I gave it different titles each time. One time it would be Coleman Hawkins or the Benny Goodman sextet. I had a ball with it. And people were going crazy. When the station manager came down, I locked the door so he couldn't fire me. Several years later I did the same thing with the Chordettes recording of *Mr. Sandman*. Both those songs were way out of my field. I think it helped make the song a hit.

I sure hope I made a difference to a lot of disc jockeys and the way radio shows were presented. I like to think of myself as a pioneer. I played the great music of the time when music had some guts and expression. Jazz is improvisation, just like my shows. Jazz and I got along. And I'm still doing it one night a week at KCSM, FM 91 at San Mateo and it's for three hours at a clip from 9 PM until midnight. I still have a legion of listeners. I hope you were one then, and maybe still one today. Come on down to the Purple Grotto. You can hear Peggy Lee, Ella, Dinah, Doris, Keely, Helen Forrest, and all those other ladies who've been around all these years singing with all those other cats I know.

Al "Jazzbeaux" Collins
February, 1997.

The 1996 Pied Pipers. Bruce Baggett, Roland Michaud, Warren Covington, Nancy Knorr and Mike Jackson. (Courtesy Warren Covington)

18

THE PIED PIPERS

by Warren Covington with Nancy Knorr

It seems that everyone wants to know about the greatest of all vocal groups, The Pied Pipers. Richard Grudens asked me and the newest leader of the group to compose this short chapter about the outstanding performers whose work has inspired listeners to continue to appreciate the wonderful arrangements and interpretations of some of the best songs ever written.

I have always been involved with the Pied Pipers in one way or another throughout my music career as both trombonist and band leader. I have known Nancy since she was twelve. Now that I have retired, Nancy has become the leader and lead singer of the wonderful Pied Pipers. It couldn't be in better hands.

Of course, the Pipers were around even before Jo Stafford joined the once all-male singing group back in the California movie studio days. The original members were John Huddleston, Chuck Lowry, Hal Hopper, Woody Newbury, Whit Whittinghill, Bud Harvey, and John Tait. It became an octet with the addition of Jo Stafford.

The group came to the attention of the public while performing on the Raleigh-Kool radio show in 1938, when Tommy Dorsey hired the group to sing with his band. Because he could not afford to pay eight singers, Tommy let them go after the show, which bombed anyway since the band performed songs the English sponsor just didn't like. When the group re-emerged as a quartet—three guys and a gal, Tommy reconsidered and re-hired them. The group was now composed of Jo, Lowrey, Yocum, and Huddleston.

While with Tommy Dorsey, the Pipers sometimes backed singers Connie Haines, Frank Sinatra, and later Dick Haymes, especially on specialty songs and recordings. Frank would always do his best to work harmonically with the group. Jo was a very cool and calm singer, but always considered herself simply the distaff member

19

although she sang lead. Their first and biggest hit *I'll Never Smile Again*, was written by Ruth Lowe who, while mourning the loss of her husband, was inspired to compose the song. *Oh! Look At Me Now* was another big hit, written by pianist Joe Bushkin and included our friend Connie Haines and Frank Sinatra.

During that time the Pipers and Dorsey made the movies *Ship Ahoy* and *DuBarry Was A Lady* for MGM with Frank Sinatra, Jo Stafford, Buddy Rich and Ziggy Elman as stars. The Pipers remained with Dorsey for two years, 1940 to 1942.

The Pipers began working with Johnny Mercer, becoming the first artists to sign with his newly-formed Capitol Records. That recording and now Piper theme song *Dream* won the first Gold Record for Capitol and the Pipers and was featured on their *Chesterfield Music Shop* radio show.

They performed with Frank Sinatra on the Lucky Strike program *Your Hit Parade*. In 1944 June Hutton, bandleader Ina Ray Hutton's younger sister and wife of arranger Axel Stordahl, replaced Jo Stafford who left to go on her own at the urging of Johnny Mercer who wanted her to record solo for Capitol. She had just married Capitol arranger and leader Paul Weston.

The Pipers with June, who remained for four years, appeared in the film *Make Mine Music* in 1946. When Tommy Dorsey suddenly died in his sleep on November 26, 1956, Willard Alexander, head of the booking agency that bore his name, called upon me to front the Tommy Dorsey Band which I did until 1962. At that time the Pipers were simply composed of various studio singers.

In the Seventies, because of my association with Tommy Dorsey's great band, I was asked to organize a "salute" to Tommy and include a vocal group like the Pipers. Researching ownership of the Pied Pipers, I learned that no one had retained rights so I was able to obtain ownership through properly registering copyrights and trademarks. The smooth sounds of the Pied Pipers were alive once again.

At one time Lillian Clark Oliver, one of the Clark Sisters and Sy Oliver's wife, performed with the Pipers for a while, as did lead singer Lynn Roberts, Tommy's former solo Song Star.

During the Eighties and right up to today, the Pipers still play "gigs" at showcases everywhere in the U.S. with Big Bands like

Tommy Dorsey (under Buddy Morrow's direction), Tex Beneke, and Jimmy Dorsey's estate band under Jim Miller's able baton. Of course, personnel in the Pipers has revolved throughout the years. The group today is composed of singers Nancy Knorr, Michael Jackson (the one with the *other* glove), Roland Michaud, and Scott Whitfield. Some of our best performances have been *I'll Never Smile Again, Sunny Side of the Street, At Last, Dream, There Are Such Things, Street of Dreams,* and *Oh, Look at Me Now,* all perennial favorites and all done in the same unique, original arrangements. Recently, the Pipers with Nancy were featured performers on a PBS special entitled *Those Fabulous Forties.*

The Pipers still have millions of fans. They wrote the magic book on singing groups. Their timeless songs and the nostalgia evoked by those memories keep the Pied Pipers music going and going.

Warren Covington

January, 1997

Author's Note: Warren Covington, originally with the bands of Isham Jones, Mitchell Ayres and Les Brown (Warren's trombone worked on the great recording *I've Got My Love to Keep Me Warm),* took over Tommy Dorsey's baton and continued the tradition. Warren is considered a brilliant lead trombone player and has worked with a "who's who" in music including Horace Heidt, Gene Krupa, and my friend Johnny Mince. He worked on shows with Arthur Godfrey, Perry Como, and Ed Sullivan and developed the sound track of the film *The Godfather.*

Warren is the author of several *Billboard* award-winning songs-among them *Miss July* and *Waltzing Trombones.*

Nancy Knorr, a Song Star in her own right with her own unique style, has been a classical musician, playing viola with the St.Louis Philharmonic Orchestra and in many chamber groups. As a vocalist Nancy has performed over the years with the Tommy Dorsey Orchestra, Les Brown's Band of Renown, and Tex Beneke's band, as well as the Warren Covington and Jimmy Dorsey bands. As Pied Piper proprietor and lead singer, Nancy continues to tour and also solos with Jim Miller's Jimmy Dorsey Band, helping, as with the Pipers, to recreate the elegance and sound of America's greatest music.

Bessie Smith awaits her cue. (Photo Rudi Blesh). 1920.

IN THE BEGINNING

A Tribute from Bessie Smith to Ella Fitzgerald

In the beginning God made Heaven and Earth and then, in a wild, extraordinary moment, added the powerful vocal influences of Ma "Gertrude" Rainey, Bessie Smith, Mildred Bailey, Ethel Waters, Billie Holiday, Ella Fitzgerald, and Dinah Washington. What a magnificent cornucopia of great jazz voices.

MA RAINEY AND BESSIE SMITH

In 1923 Ma "Gertrude" Rainey, an absolute original Song Star, was the undisputed top blues singer. A genuine diva, she was known in those pioneer days as The Mother of the Blues, who shouted and moaned the laments of her life's condition. They say that one day she came to the town of Chattanooga, Tennessee, heard Bessie Smith and took her in tow as a member of her famous traveling blues troupe. Legend has it that Ma Rainey literally kidnapped Bessie at the age of twelve, forcing the girl to go with her show, teaching her how to sing the blues, Ma Rainey style; but that was denied later by those who really knew. Actually, they got along fine, but Bessie never learned much about singing from Rainey's troupe. She was a natural singer and her own person who learned all aspects of her craft. She could Charleston and do funny turns, then send an audience into a trance with her shy, but earthy blues. Rainey was more like a mother than a teacher to Bessie Smith. Remember, too, history will bear out there was just no blues predecessor to Ma Rainey.

Historically, for unknown reasons, female blues singers followed male blues singers. "Bessie Smith, had she lived a full life, would have been right there on top with the rest of us in the Swing Era," Lionel Hampton opined during our interview about the great female singers. She was known as the 'Empress Of The Blues.'" With a raucous and loud voice, a complete command of a lyric and the ability to bring first-hand emotion to a song, there was misery in what she did, but some say she just had to bring it all out in her music.

The post World War I period brought the blues north. By the early 1920's, Bessie Smith was a recording and performing giant, two hundred pounds of human emotion packed behind her vibrant, powerful voice. She made over 150 records and was so successful that her record sales literally saved Columbia Records from bankruptcy, even though they had voices like Eddie Cantor and Al Jolson in their stable. Her record sales surpassed a stupendous 10 million in a time when there were relatively few phonographs and little available money for the average person to purchase them. Along the way she earned a great deal of money, at one time making two thousand dollars a week, but, just as easily, lost it all. She gave it away or spent it on liquor, or lost it to men predators.

There was magic in her voice. Some say her songs represented the common man in his sorrow and sometimes terrible condition. The main themes of her songs were love, sex, and misery. The recordings *Sorrowful Blues* and *Rocking Chair Blues* were promoted heavily by Columbia. Magazine and newspaper ads in 1924 read: "Having a phonograph without these records is like having ham without eggs." Louis Armstrong recorded with Bessie when he was only twenty-four years old and fresh from King Oliver's Creole Jazz Band in Chicago. He joined Fletcher Henderson's orchestra and, with Bessie, he had met his match: He later said: "She thrilled me always. She had music in her soul." That recording date, January 14, 1925, although not important at the time, would, for critics and scholars, stand as a memorable date in jazz history. The session started with W. C. Handy's endlessly recorded *St.Louis Blues*, and became the definitive recording. The selections on the rest of the session, *Reckless Blues, Cold in Hand Blues,* and *Sobbin' Hearted Blues*, all became classics, attesting to her greatness.

By the 1930's good blues singers' popularity began diminishing, falling behind the proliferating jazz singers who were out working the scene. Bessie saw the day when Ethel Waters' more sophisticated torch singing pushed her off the boards. Bessie went down—still trouping. Her untimely death at the age of forty-one in a September, 1937 automobile accident virtually coincided with the renaissance of traditional jazz that began in the late thirties. By 1938 Columbia released the first Bessie Smith reissues, a new generation of blues women began to record, and Bessie was already becoming a legend. If she had lived, imagine her singing with the great locomotive band of Count Basie. It would have been something to hear.

ETHEL WATERS

Ethel Waters lived several musical lives. She started out in black vaudeville as a long-legged dancer and singer known as Sweet Mama Stringbean. One of the first black singers to be accepted on the same level with white singers, Ethel Waters was first to demonstrate the many possibilities for jazz singing in good commercial tunes. As an example, she made the first recording of the immensely popular *Dinah*, later performed by many other notables including Bing Crosby. Although her style was different from Bessie Smith's, Ethel had an enormous personality and talent, but it was difficult for her to compete with Bessie Smith the star.

In 1932 and '33, Ethel Waters recorded with Duke Ellington, along with a group of other well-established singers like the Mills Brothers, performing selections from all-black revues, including the *Blackbirds of 1933*. Her rendition of *I Can't Give You Anything But Love,* recorded with Ellington in 1932, is the definitive version, eclipsing that of Aida Ward's in 1928. Ethel also recorded with Benny Carter and Teddy Wilson earning respectability even as a Bessie Smith-type blues singer. When beginning her stage appearances, she devised a cute opening where someone off stage would ask, "Are you Ethel Waters?" and she'd answer, "Well, I ain't Bessie Smith." It would excite the audience and then she would break out with a heart-breaking blues number.

Ethel Waters was also a remarkable lady of the theater. From early childhood she envisioned herself a great actress. Her later celebrity as an actress eclipsed her importance as an accomplished singer of the blues. Along with Bessie and Louis, she shone as a dis-

25

Ethel Waters (Circa 1940.)
(Richard Grudens Collection)

tinctive singer of her time. She considered Ma Rainey and Bessie Smith and other blues singers as shouters. Her acceptance by the public was due to an advised change in her repertoire. Stepping away from Smith-like songs, she adopted songs other than blues. Although she never could read music, she would say, "My music is all queer little things that come into my head. All queer things that I hum."

This led to engagements at the Cotton Club in Harlem and the Plantation Club on Broadway, to recording sessions with Jimmy and Tommy Dorsey, Benny Goodman and many more, and finally to the movies notably *As Thousands Cheer* in 1933 and *Cabin In The Sky* in 1940, where she sang her unexpected success *Taking A Chance On Love*, thereby achieving success as both singer and actress. Her rendition of *I Can't Give You Anything But Love* with the Duke Ellington orchestra in 1932 is the most enduring version on record. On the second chorus of this recording, she almost sounds like a man, the voice lowdown and bluesy. Find a copy if you love early jazz/blues prizes.

Ethel Waters, a blues singer, jazz singer, actress, and riveting personality, could swing in the jazz idiom of the times. In the book *The Real Jazz*, author Hugues Panassie wraps it up accordingly: "Her voice, although a miracle of smoothness, is nonetheless firm and penetrating, clear and supple, swinging, caressing, cynical, with myriads of little touches and inflections....since 1930 she had been influenced to some degree by Louis Armstrong. As a matter of fact, Ethel Waters' influence on female jazz singers is almost as great as that of Louis Armstrong." Later, Ethel Waters became a star of the religious world when she traveled and preached with the Reverend Billy Graham's troupe.

MILDRED BAILEY

Mildred Bailey was an immensely successful singer of the newly established Swing Era with her particular mastery of phrasing. Part Couer d'Alene Indian, she was xylophonist (not vibes) Red Norvo's wife and later sang with his band. She credited her Indian heritage for the unusual quality of her high-pitched tone, which balanced her warm lower range.

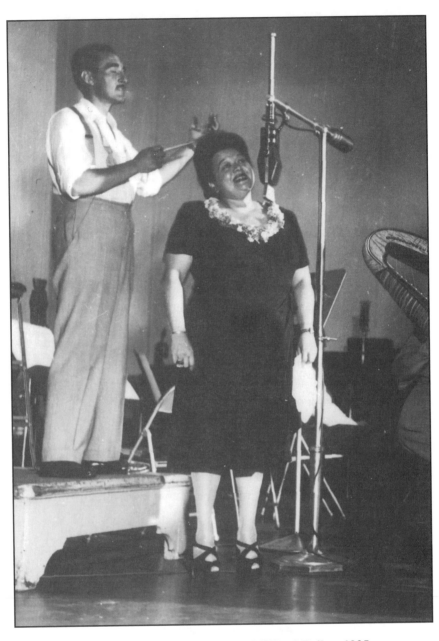

The first Girl Big Band singer Mildred Bailey. 1935.
(Richard Grudens Collection)

After running away from home because her father re-married after her Mother died, Mildred originally got in the music business in Seattle, Washington. "She had a job demonstrating sheet music in a ten cents-a-copy music store. She played piano and sang each song for customers," The eighty-nine year old Red said in a conversation I had with him just yesterday. "She had an excellent memory. Before a recording date she would go over a song once or twice with me at home and simply memorized it. She always recorded in one take.

"In the 1930's Mildred had her own NBC radio show on Monday, Wednesday, and Friday nights for 15 minutes. That's where I first met her—I was backing her," Red said.

Mildred Bailey and Red Norvo were known as Mr. and Mrs. Swing, a sobriquet levied on them by George Simon in his column for Metronome magazine. With Norvo and pianist-bandleader Teddy Wilson of Benny Goodman Quartet fame, Mildred waxed some great recordings. Her recordings of *Melancholy Baby, A Lull In My Life,* and *Russian Lullaby* (a little known tune but a favorite with jazz performers) are the best examples of her superiority in the genre. *Rockin'Chair,* Hoagy Carmichael's evergreen classic, became a hit and was always identified as Mildred's own. "She used it as a theme song," Red said. It was a variation of the blues, although somewhat closer to the new swing patterns.

"Hoagy used to hang around on the movie set *King of Jazz* (Paul Whiteman and Bing Crosby's landmark film). He wanted Mildred to introduce the song because he thought she could sing it better than anyone else," Red said. Mildred became known as the "Rockin' Chair Lady." "Her recording of *Lazy Bones*—you know, Johnny Mercer's tune—he was her friend and she always did his tunes—and *More Than You Know* were her best recordings as far as I'm concerned."

Mildred Bailey remains one of the finest jazz vocalists of the era. "She possessed a clear voice and excellent diction (*a' la* Frank Sinatra) and vocalized with conviction and warmth. Her diction was so exceptional," Red reiterated. Again, like the later Sinatra, she consciously surrounded herself with the best musicians available.

Red Norvo and others, too, have said that with her recording of *Rockin Chair*, Mildred Bailey became the very first *girl singer* of the Big Bands. Credit for this goes to the uncanny ability and foresight of

Brunswick Records A & R man Jack Kapp (later he went with Decca and worked with Bing Crosby and was responsible for the success of the Andrews Sisters, Rosemary Clooney, Tony Bennett, and other great vocalists). Mildred was Al Rinker's sister. Al was one of Bing Crosby's original singing partners in the Rhythm Boys singing group along with Harry Barris It was Mildred who encouraged the three friends to come to Hollywood. The rest, as they say, is history. Many years later Mildred appeared with Bing Crosby on his landmark radio show in L.A. in 1950 and together they sang *I've Got The World On A String*, just like in the earlier Paul Whiteman days.

Mildred died in 1951 in a Poughkeepsie, New York, hospital, not far from her upstate New York farm. She had retired in 1949. Mildred Bailey, although mostly unknown to the modern world, was the catalyst for many singers including Frank Sinatra. Tony Bennett told me in no uncertain terms that it was Mildred Bailey who influenced his singing career the most as did Frankie Laine. "Bing told me many times that he learned to sing from Mildred," Red proudly declared. In his autobiography *Call Me Lucky*, Bing said, "I was lucky in knowing the great jazz and blues singer Mildred Bailey so early in life. She taught me so much about singing and about interpreting popular songs."

And, there is this little-known story: "She was responsible for discovering Billie Holiday along with John Hammond," Red recalled, "They were up on the second floor of the Apollo (Theater in New York) where the white people sat, when Billie appeared on stage in an amateur show, and Mildred excitedly said, 'That girl can sing!' and ran downstairs to find out her name."

Take a moment one quiet day and put Mildred Bailey's records on the turntable and simply listen.

BILLIE HOLIDAY

When it comes to improvisation, it's a rule that the singer must keep the song recognizable. The lyrics can stray off the melody line but must arrive back on track by the end of a phrase. Billie Holiday was the master of this kind of singing. If Bessie Smith's example enno-

Billie Holiday, *New York Daily News* advertisement, June 7, 1946.
(Richard Grudens Collection)

The mature Billie Holiday tells her story.
(Richard Grudens Collection)

bled a tradition, Billie was the singer whose life spelled out that tradition. "It's not a matter of what you do, but how you do it," Fats Waller once declared. Billie Holiday's recording of *What A Little Moonlight Can Do* with Teddy Wilson clearly demonstrates this musical necessity. Here a plain song takes on jazz expressions of major proportions. Billie's best recordings, I believe, were made with pianist and bandleader Teddy Wilson. "She made the most beautiful records with her friend Lester Young, when she recorded with me back in the thirties," Teddy Wilson personally told me back in 1982. Lester Young's tenor sax suited Billie Holiday perfectly. Her voice was also her instrument. Like Bing Crosby, Billie skillfully took advantage of the advent of the microphone, using her supple, sensitive voice to embrace it, delivering a song in a totally different way than when not using the microphone. Remember that Billie was not a blues singer, as 95% of her recordings were not blues by any account.

In later years Billie's voice became a mere shadow of her greater days. The voice and spirit was worn and sounded old. Her stressed life of drugs and abuse, heaped upon her mostly by others, ended in an early death at forty-four. There was no doubt as to Billie Holiday's credentials as a major, influential jazz voice of the 20th century. Almost every vocalist who followed, male and female, acknowledged their debt to the quintessential jazz singer Billie Holiday. Here we are in February 1997, and Tony Bennett, at 70 years, has recorded an album entitled: *Tony Bennett: On Holiday*, a tribute recording where the magic of modern electronics permits Tony to sing a duet with Billie—*God Bless The Child*. He's earned the right.

ELLA FITZGERALD

After Holiday there was a host of female singers performing on the swing circuit. You can never say too much about the success that was Ella Jane Fitzgerald. So much has been written about Ella who was really a contemporary of Billie Holiday and also rates as one of the best voices of the *Jazz Age*. Growing up, she absorbed the sounds of Connee Boswell and the Boswell Sisters, Bing Crosby, and Louis Armstrong. Her big hit with the Chick Webb band that led her to the big

The Great Ella Fitzgerald 1950.
(Richard Grudens Collection)

time was *A Tisket, A-Tasket*. It was a late 1930's swinging, pouty version of an otherwise dull song and an auspicious beginning for the talented teenager. Shortly after her mother died, Chick Webb actually rescued Ella from a fate in an orphanage by adopting her as his own daughter. Ella was a somewhat gawky, rather unruly—scarsely chic—bandstand singer. But it was her voice that appealed to Webb.

In the forties, Ella scored with *How High The Moon* and George Gershwin's *Lady Be Good*, both durable Swing Era favorites and a prelude to her scat vocals, leading jazz straight into bebop by the late 1940's. She was the prototypical swing singer. "She uses the blues structure when she improvises: she can hum a blues languidly or drive it joyously through fast tempo and melody changes," said Stuart Nicholson in his recent biography of Ella. Her story is strikingly opposite Billie's. Although both were initially handicapped by poverty and race, the difference was temperament and personal strength. There was no alcohol, addiction, or degradation. Ella Fitzgerald was constantly amazed at her fame. A somewhat nervous performer, she was never at home with interviews or publicity even up to the end. I know about that very well. I once had an opportunity to interview Ella, but, as luck would have it, a terrible snow storm prevented me from traveling the twenty-five miles to the theater that appointed evening. I never got a second chance. And believe me, I tried.

The *Songbook* albums produced by her manager and producer since the 1950's, Norman Granz, were great individual albums and definitive interpretations of songwriters George Gershwin (the best of them-it contains the best version of *Of Thee I Sing* ever done), Jerome Kern, Cole Porter, Harold Arlen, and Irving Berlin. They are considered lasting treasures of American music. They are all so exceptional. William B. Williams, legendary host of New York's WNEW's *Make Believe Ballroom* for many years, called Ella the "First Lady of Song," or sometimes just plain *Ella*. As Leonard Feather astutely observed in his 1972 book, *From Satchmo to Miles*: "Ella Fitzgerald is one of the most flexible, beautiful, and widely appreciated voices of this century."

Her thirteen Grammy Awards started with the 1958 Best Vocal Performance, *Ella Fitzgerald Sings The Irving Berlin Songbook*, to the 1990 Best Jazz Vocal Performance for *All That Jazz*. She has been honored with honorary doctorates at both Yale and Dartmouth Universities.

Accepting the Yale award, she said with characteristic modesty, "Not bad for someone who only studied music to get that half-credit in high school." In 1979 she received a Kennedy Center Honors Award.

During her final days, her old friend Bea Wain, a wonderful Song Star herself with those treasured recordings *Deep Purple* and *My Reverie* recorded with Larry Clinton, went driving around town together with Ella and her chauffeur. "It was April 25 and it was Ella's 78th birthday. Our mutual friend Joyce Garro and I were at her home celebrating her special day. We were laughing, singing and eating birthday cake. We reminisced about our past, beginning in the latter part of 1937 when I was singing with Larry Clinton and she was with Chick Webb. Although she was ill, Ella usually went for a ride in her big beautiful car every day. On this day she invited me to come along. She sat in the front with her driver and I was in the rear with her nurse. The radio was tuned to one of the jazz stations and, of course, we were listening to Ella coming over the air. She sang along with herself and clapped her hands in time. She called out the names of some of the musicians and remembered them really well. I have to say that the ride with Ella on her last birthday was a tremendous thrill. I loved her so much and I miss her so...."

A tribute was held at Carnegie Hall on Tuesday, July 9, 1996 to celebrate the life and career of Ella Fitzgerald. Margaret Whiting, Bobby Short, John Pizzarelli, Harry "Sweets" Edison, Lionel Hampton, Ruth Brown, Herb Ellis, Jack Jones, Diana Krall, and Chris Conner were there contributing through song. It was narrated by Jonathan Schwartz, the excellent disc jockey of New York's newly re-vamped radio station WQEW, the most listened to radio station playing standards in the United States. It was intended to be a testimonial to a living legend, but wound up as a fitting eulogy to the excellence of Song Star Ella Fitzgerald.

And Furthermore

Notably, and assuredly, America's finest popular music was written in the first half of this century and performed in excellence by those singers chronicled in this and the ensuing chapters. The works of

Harold Arlen, Irving Berlin, Cole Porter, Jerome Kern, Rodgers and Hart, Johnny Mercer, Billy Strayhorn, Duke Ellington and some notable others are responsible for that truth. But, what value were those strains without their transmitters, the vocalists who ultimately delivered the goods?

Cole Porter's *Night and Day* has been performed over and over and recorded by dozens of singers, but the singer Sinatra possesses the song. Kitty Kallen owns Franklyn Stutz/Edith Calisch's *Little Things Mean a Lot* just as much as Tony Bennett holds the deed to *I Left My Heart In San Francisco*. Oh, others sing them, but who's listening? And doesn't Kate Smith occupy the monument that is Irving Berlin's *God Bless America*?

Harold Arlen wrote the song *Over The Rainbow* for Judy Garland's performance in the film *The Wizard Of Oz*. Would the song have been composed differently if they had selected a different performer? Could anyone but Ethel Merman have put across Jerry Herman's *Everything's Coming Up Roses* as definitively? And how many songs does America's most prolific singer, Bing Crosby, personify? Hundreds, at least! And how about Al Jolson's *Mammy*, or *Swanee*. Well, you know what I mean.

Today's singers are out there interpreting songs from the pens of more recent songwriters, Paul Simon, Burt Bacharach, John Lennon and Paul McCartney, Henry Mancini, Kris Kristofferson, Randy Newman, Paul Williams, and others. The songs are, for the most part, not as memorable, although good enough. They were also not as up-front as their vintage counterparts. Today, Top Forty hits are mostly rock and roll ditties that defy the gravity of good music. During the '30's, '40's, and '50's, it was quite different. All songwriters participated in producing the compositions we now define as "standards." It is, as Tony Bennett explained to me, "America's classical music."

So as fine as a song can be, and there are so many to consider, it ultimately takes orchestra and vocalist to commit it to fame and posterity. Ma Rainey, Bessie Smith, Ella Fitzgerald, Dinah Washington, Mildred Bailey, Ethel Waters, and Billie Holiday were some of those singers. Each was one-of-a-kind, who more than adequately filled the voids during America's great Golden Age Of Music through her own imagination and ingenious artistry.

**Josephine Baker in her famous banana costume in Paris. 1936.
(Richard Grudens Collection)**

JOSEPHINE BAKER

A Different Song Star

Most Big Band enthusiasts have left Josephine Baker out of their collective hearts, but I feel that she deserves a chapter of her own. Josephine Baker was a supreme Song Star and dynamic entertainer who enjoyed most of her greater moments in Europe because of race rejection in the U.S. during World War II and before. An extraordinary entertainer born to a black mother and a Jewish father, she added exotic touches to her singing. She exploded on stage in extravagant regalia.

Her early dream was to become successful in America, but realized it finally in Europe, becoming intimate friends of European royalty, nobility, presidents, and even dictators, although her somewhat scandalous and spirited stage image was a strong contrast to anything she would be able to do in America. Every major designer in Paris fought for the privilege of clothing Miss Baker including Poiret, Patou, Chanel and Schiaparelli, then Dior and Balmain. Upon her death, she was honored by a 21-gun salute French state funeral.

While researching the life of Josephine Baker, I was talking one day with singer Frankie Laine who knew Max Wirz, a Swiss disc-jockey who currently emcees an American Song Star show in Switzerland and is a friend to both Frankie Laine and Big Band Jump's host Don Kennedy. I was able to reach Max and queried him about anyone in Europe who might have known Miss Baker during World War II when she was active in the French Resistance. Max linked me to André Doudot also from Switzerland who, as a young man, knew Josephine Baker during the War years. His father (later awarded the American Medal Of Freedom with bronze palm and citation) belonged to the French Intelligence Service and consequently they all had to hide in Morocco under pseudonyms.

"To the best I can remember," he said in a letter he sent along with four never-before published photographs of Josephine Baker, "these photos, taken in Morocco, took place one year after my family had escaped from occupied France. One evening, my father told my mother: 'The operation was successful......you should pay *her* a visit at the clinic and make sure *she* has all her needs.' Obviously my mother knew who he was talking about. My question came logically: 'Who do we visit?' My father's answer: 'Josephine Baker.' My father was not joking, I concluded. Learning the rules of silence in those days, I asked no further questions.

"We went to the clinic the following day (clinque Comte' located on Boulevard de la Marne') and we were brought to Josephine Baker's room. Her name was not on the door. My mother greeted her and introduced me, saying 'This is André,' " he continued his interesting story, "I walked towards the bed and kissed her hand the way I had been taught. Josephine was moved. And the star, the goddess to

Capt. Abtey, Mrs. Doudot, Josephine Baker, Marie Doudot. 1943—Morocco, Africa. (André Doudot Collection)

40

my eyes, spoke, not like a star or a goddess: 'Well, here is this young man I have heard about!' She inquired about my studies, what kind of books or authors. In a matter of minutes I had forgotten she was the world famous singer and dancer. I was amazed by so much simplicity and kindness. Her French was fairly fluent with a delightful accent.

"Sometimes later, after her convalescence, she came to our house often and had lunch. She brought a number of books for me and my sister. A simple meal, I remember my mother had prepared a chicken which seemed to be her favorite plate. I overcame my shyness and asked if I could take a few photographs outside in a small garden. She accepted willingly. Everyone left the table, including our maid and her baby. I had only four pictures left in the camera and here they are..."

This story is confirmed in Josephine Baker's autobiography *Josephine*. Accordingly, it seems that the Captain Abtey in the photo was actually Sub-lieutenant Baker's superior officer in the French Resistance. He had just promoted her from Lieutenant, her admitted fondest memory of the War. Her duration in the clinic was an operation for an infection probably sprung from an injection she had received. It was a long convalescence. Her sickroom became a perfect rendezvous spot for Resistance members. She relapsed with peritonitis and continued ill and weak for several more months. The Doudots were the family near the clinic who took her in while she was convalescing. Josephine was awarded the prestigious Medal of Resistance by General Charles de Gaulle for her work during World War II.

This future legend came long way from a black ghetto in St. Louis where she was born in 1903 (some say 1906). Her father, Eddie Carson, was a drummer; her mother, Carrie MacDonald, an amateur dancer and waitress. The better part of her young life was spent as a maid scrubbing floors, peeling potatoes, and washing clothes for wealthy whites.

Josephine Baker was known internationally for her fabulously elaborate gowns and headdresses, receiving standing ovations at the Folies-Bergere after introducing *le jazz hot* to Paris in *La Revue Ne'-gre* in 1925. She was known there as the "Dark Star." Her short Big Band affiliation was with Noble Sissle and Eubie Blake, touring with other beginners Florence Mills and Paul Robeson in a show called

Shuffle which was renamed *Chocolate Dandies*, when the show got to New York. Appearing at the famed Plantation club in Greenwich Village along with Song Star Ethel Waters, Josephine sang Ethel's repertoire one night solo when Ethel took sick, notably rousing renditions of *Dinah*, Ethel's best known tune, and *Charleston*.

"It brought down the house and even though I didn't sing it as well as Ethel—I'd never been really taught to do *that*, either." stated Josephine. She left for Paris shortly after that day where she made a tremendous impact and was a fashionable rage for months. The French had a growing obsession with black entertainment.

Pre-dating her prodigious Folies-Bergere appearances, Josephine also worked with Eddy Howard, who became her musical director in Europe for one year. He later returned to the U.S. to form his own Big Band. She was also affiliated with Claude Hopkins, who led a popular black band in America and went on to perform with Josephine's nearly nude dancing show in the *Revue Ne`gre* at the Champs-Elysees Music Hall in Paris. Here she appeared with two cheetahs and dressed only in a girdle of imitation bananas and a few feathers. Josephine's magnificently athletic body was a major asset, but she also had a very personal way with a song, spontaneous and fickle, and a stage personality that was magnetic and laid back. On her return to Paris, after her rejection by New York audiences in the Zeigfield Follies of 1936, Josephine appeared with world famous performer Maurice Chevalier. She became a French citizen in 1937.

After the war, Josephine took over a home for refugee children and ran it with her husband and conductor Jo Bouillon. They adopted twelve children of different races, a monument in itself. Actress Grace Kelly (by then Princess Grace) helped provide a house near Monaco for Josephine, her twelve adopted children that she christened her "rainbow tribe," and her sister. Grace had always admired Josephine's courage in the face of adversity.

She returned to the stage in Paris at the Olympia Theater in 1966 and later in the French production of *Hello Dolly* in 1968. In Europe Josephine remained a figure of enormous popularity. In 1975 a final gala show to celebrate 50 years in entertainment was performed at the Bobino Music Hall in London.

Josephine Baker was indeed a gigantic living monument, composed of talent and courage. Future generations of blacks throughout America have benefited from her trailblazing, their road made easier through her lifelong fight against racism. I'm glad I ran into André Doudot, who is now my friend and *Song Star* collaborator.

1940's Helen Forrest.
(Richard Grudens Collection)

HELEN FORREST

Voice of the Big Bands

Once upon a Big Band time, Helen Fogel, a very young girl from Atlantic City, New Jersey, sang her heart out regularly on New York radio station WNEW for very little pay. In those days some radio shows were labeled "sustaining," meaning the show had no sponsor and, consequently, low-pay for performers. But they aired anyway. Helen wasn't worried because the exposure eventually led to a salaried CBS Network job vocalizing alongside trumpeter Bunny Berigan (famous later for his top recording of the era, *I Can't Get Started*). Fortunately, bandleader Artie Shaw heard her one night at the Madrillon Club in Washington, D.C. and promptly contacted Helen to ask her to sing with his band. Although Billie Holiday was the current featured singer with the Shaw band, she was weary of the racist treatment received on the road despite the best efforts of the concerned bandleader and decided to quit. Billie, the only black performer in the all-white Shaw band, had to endure degrading racial indignities quite common in those days.

Recalling her friend Billie Holiday, Helen said: "Billie was just wonderful to me. Always trying to help, she used to tell Artie to let me sing some of her songs. She was really a great, caring person." During the following year or so, 21 year old Helen recorded 38 singles with Shaw at RCA's New York studios. The year was 1939 and the Big Band Era was now in full swing, thanks to earlier groundbreakers Benny Goodman and Glenn Miller.

Helen Fogel, now known to everyone as Helen Forrest, was appearing professionally being recognized as the best singer Shaw ever had. Helen learned to dramatize a song: "I try to sing so a guy can picture soft lights and his girl," Helen told a *Look Magazine*

45

interviewer back in 1944. Her voice always evoked excitement and emotion.

Helen skipped over to Benny Goodman's band after Artie Shaw suddenly disbanded his organization in late 1939 by suddenly walking off the bandstand at a hotel where he was performing. Joe Graydon, Helen's friend and personal manager for over 45 years, explained that it was because Artie was apparently unable to endure the pressure fame had brought him, "and he thoroughly disliked his audiences." Joe added, "He summoned the band to his room and told them that he was through and offered the band to Helen or (valued sideman) Tony Pastor."

Later, Shaw explained that he considered the whole music business a "racket" and moved to Mexico. But in less than a year, he was back and busier than ever.

Helen had no problem at all finding work: "Benny said I was *his* singer." Helen told me, "I didn't even have to audition....but I had to take a pay cut from $175.00 a week to $85.00. I took it because I wanted to work with Benny's band even though Benny once said I couldn't sing. Benny really didn't care much about singers anyway."

Helen sang some distinctive, early Eddie Sauter quality arrangements including *Darn That Dream*, her first and perhaps best Goodman recording. *The Man I Love*, another Sauter arrangement, highlighted by Helen's special vocalizing techniques, is further proof of her ability to deliver fresh melodic textures unexpectedly. Helen was fortunate in the reality that Eddie Sauter wrote such worthy arrangements, giving her more room than is customary when girl singers are constricted by the limitations of dance band tempos. Despite this, she managed to skillfully shade a song and project her personality into her singing successfully. In August of 1941, Helen suddenly quit the Goodman band ("to avoid having a nervous breakdown," she said), paving the way for sultry Peggy Lee. In 1940, I should add, Helen recorded *Ghost of a Chance* with Lionel Hampton and the Nat "King" Cole trio.

Helen had always admired the way Harry James played the trumpet, "So I thought I'd fit in perfectly with the band. I contacted Harry on a hunch. Peewee Monte, Harry's manager, had me come over to sing at a rehearsal, and after that Harry asked the guys in the band to take a vote and they decided they wanted me. So Harry agreed," she revealed.

In retrospect, my all time personal favorite recording of that period turned out to be the lyrical gem *I Had the Craziest Dream,* a lushly sentimental Helen Forrest performance from the Betty Grable, John Payne film *Springtime in the Rockies,* in which Helen appeared as the vocalist with Betty's soon to be real-life husband, trumpet-playing Harry James, and his Orchestra. It affected me two-fold: One, I was an impressionable young man attending a glitzy, palatial Loew's Movie Theater to see the amazing new technicolor film technology for the first time. And two, my newest hero, Harry James, was playing at his personal best on a big screen. The combination of Harry James' trumpet and Helen Forrest's voice capped off a memorable summer Sunday afternoon. But, unknown to many, the making of that movie also adversely affected Helen Forrest's relationship with James, as they were lovers and approaching marriage until Betty Grable entered the picture. For my money, that celluloid clip still stands as one of the best musical moments ever portrayed on film. That latter fact was mutually agreed upon during an interview with Harry James in 1984 when we recalled that recording's special moment: "I think it was one of my best moments, too," Harry said, but would not talk about the former, his crumbling relationship with Helen that caused her to leave him and his band.

It was during her tenure with Harry James that Helen recorded her best-known standards just as *Billboard* began publishing charts: *I've Heard That Song Before* (an incredible 13 weeks as the number—one song on the list), *I Don't Want to Walk Without You, Skylark, Mr. Five by Five* and others, all great wartime favorites. In the film *Shine On Harvest Moon*, she sang the haunting *Time Waits for No One*. Just listen to it carefully. She infuses the song with rich sentimental messages. She believes what she sings.

It seems that Harry James' band provided extraordinary support for the young singer's talents, and his arrangers enhanced those performances by interjecting nontraditional violins and capitalizing on her unique presence, much like Duke Ellington achieved showcasing individual musicians. Now, not just a girl band singer accompanying a dance number, Helen developed definitive patterns of delivery which were more individually expressive than most vocalists of her time. She favored the orchestral settings that best fit her crying kind of style. Arrangements were built around Harry's horn and Helen's voice. Remember Helen's heartbreaking rendition of *I Cried for You* in the film *Bathing Beauty* with Harry? What a delivery.

Then Helen teamed up with song stylist Dick Haymes, recognized internationally as one of the best male baritones of all time. Together, they produced six top-ten duets: *Long Ago and Far Away*, *It Had to Be You, Together, I'll Buy That Dream,* and *Oh! What It Seemed to Be.* Each of those singles sold over one million copies, Helen said. Their work was reminiscent of the memorable Big Band Era vocal combination of Bob Eberle and Helen O'Connell recorded with Jimmy Dorsey that included the popular standards *Green Eyes,* the immensely successful *Tangerine*, and *Amapola*. Helen Forrest was actually considered to be the finest white singer of the era until Tommy Dorsey's Frank Sinatra came along and upstaged her with his signature phrasing technique. It is well known that Sinatra admits he learned phrasing from observing Dorsey's trombone playing breathing techniques.

Helen ably imparted excellent phrasing, impeccable good taste, accurate pitch, and the ability to effectively shade a song. Although the influence of Mildred Bailey and Billie Holiday is clearly audible in Helen's singing, the addition of direct, sincere delivery created an extraordinary communication with her audience.

Beyond the Big Band Era, Helen earned a solid reputation in the supper-clubs, and there was heavy radio work in the '50's including her regular show with Dick Haymes. Additionally, Capitol Records revived some of her old hits in an entirely new album. While with Capitol she joined up with James once again in an album entitled *Harry James in Hi-Fi*. One of the selections was *I'm Beginning to See the Light,* a song previously recorded by Song Star Kitty Kallen.

In 1954 Helen was singing with a trio instead of a big band at a club in Long Beach, California. "To tell the truth," she said, "I did-n't go for the idea of a trio backing because it meant I couldn't use my library of big band arrangements. But Bob Braman and the boys do such a great job that now I'm more than happy. "She felt that when a small group puts their hearts into it, a singer can work with them successfully. Whenever Helen played the small clubs, she was always surprised at the big welcome she received. "I am always surprised as well as thrilled, and not only for myself but for others, because it's a sign of better things ahead for musicians and singers, as well."

In 1964 Helen toured throughout the United States (especially Las Vegas), Australia, and Britain with Frank Sinatra, Jr. and the Tommy Dorsey Orchestra. In the late Sixties she was reunited once again with James on an album entitled *20 Pieces of Harry James*, revealing that her singing techniques and ability to tear at the heartstrings was just as effective as ever.

In the late Seventies, Helen teamed with Dick Haymes, Harry James, Hildegarde, The Pied Pipers, and the Inkspots in a nostalgic revue fittingly titled *The Big Broadcast of 1944*. Helen headlined with Dick Haymes in the *Fabulous Forties* at the Parker Playhouse in November of 1978 and electrified the audience with her vocal skills. She projected a warm, gracious personality—a pairing of talent and charm. One critic said she keeps things "sparkling and fresh." All this activity worked out very well, but within four months the untimely death of Dick Haymes in March of 1980 really affected Helen.

They had been very close, having starred together on the very highly rated Autolite weekly radio show from 1944 until 1948 with Gordon Jenkins and his orchestra and the 4 Hits and a Miss singing group Thursday nights first on NBC and then on CBS. "Dick was terrific fun. He would make me laugh so hard and often that the laugh became famous," Helen said in her autobiography. "Dick thought the laughs and unexpected lines he threw at me livened up the show." They did 188 shows together, and that's a lot of shows. Helen didn't finish the shows full run, being replaced by Martha Tilton near the end in 1948. Many other Song Stars were regular guests including Betty Grable, Jo Stafford, Peggy Lee, and Dale Evans.

"Dick was one of the greatest singers of our era," Helen said, "was the finest gentleman I've ever known and a dear friend." Helen spent many hours at Dick Haymes' bedside just before he died. "It still hurts me to talk about him."

Helen Forrest sent me this photo on January 15, 1997.
(Courtesy Helen Forrest)

Helen's stroke in 1980 left Helen terrified she'd be paralyzed. For a while she couldn't walk or talk. "But I'm very lucky," she said. "I recovered. I didn't even need vocal therapy to get my voice back."

In 1983, on the Stash label, Helen performed in a jazz setting with some fine musicians including pianist-composer Hank Jones and premier bassist George Duvivier, mostly reviving a handful of her old hits produced under the title of *Sunny Side of the Street*. Audiophile records released a batch of her radio transcriptions from the 1950's with accompaniment by either Carmen Dragon or The Ray Bloch Orchestra. At that time it was Wendell Echols of *Jazzbeat* who labeled her the *Queen of the Big Band Singers* in his review of this very good CD release. Helen's latest albums are on the Hindsight Label with Carmen Dragon's orchestra.

Some people have posed the question: Why didn't Helen Forrest become a really big up-front mega-star with worldwide exposure like many of her peers? Well, she did, but in her own quiet way. Her recordings are absolute musical treasures. After all, she was a girl singer with many celebrated bands and, until the Fifties, band singers rarely starred on their own unless, as in the case of Doris Day, they were featured in high-profile movies. Sinatra was another exception, as was Frankie Laine and Perry Como, but only after going solo and only after struggling for a time. In the Thirties and Forties, the headline on the marquees' was invariably the name of the leader of the featured Big Band.

Joe Graydon told me that because of Helen's tenure with James, Goodman and Shaw, she has often been referred to as "The Voice of the Big Bands." "Another title which stuck with her was "One take Helen," he said, "because her first recording take was always great. If they had to do others, it was because of a mistake within the band." Helen has always had incredibly good intonation, which musically can be defined as regard to accuracy of pitch.

Don Kennedy, host of Big Band Jump, a nationally syndicated radio show, and editor of the Big Band Jump Newsletter, has uncompromisingly selected Helen Forrest as the finest Big Band girl singer of the era:

"Her vocals soared without losing feeling; they retained a crispness without sacrificing the emotional effect....and what are vocals for if not to affect the emotions of the listener," he went even further, "It's certainly true that the best artists of all kinds are the ones whose technique is not evident....who make it seem easy."

Helen Forrest made it seem easy.

In 1996 Helen Forrest was installed as Honorary President of the "Dick Haymes Society" which is based in England with co-organizer Roger Dooner managing the American wing from his home in Minneapolis, Minnesota. The Society distributes an excellent 100 page newsletter. Joining such a Society opens up a myriad storehouse of information about Dick Haymes, Helen Forrest, and others associated with the Big Band era. Yes, you can join if you wish. If you feel as I do about all that great music, you will receive a great lift by participating in such tributes and helping to keep the memories alive. Just give me a call one day.

I hope you like the updated photo that Helen sent me just today to grace this chapter of her life. You can see for yourself that she looks as good as she sounds.

Helen Forrest with Harry James sings *I've Heard That Song Before*.
(Richard Grudens Collection)

Kitty Kallen sings with Harry James. 1943.
(Kitty Kallen Collection)

KITTY KALLEN

Little Things Still Mean a Lot

Okay, devoted Big Band culture buffs, can you identify the young lady named Katherine who sang with the Jan Savitt Band on KYW-CBS radio in Philadelphia at the adolescent age of 14 and continued on to vocalize as the "Girl" with jazz trombonist Jack Teagarden's Orchestra, "Sixteen Men and a Girl," in 1939?

This very same young lady was featured with Jimmy Dorsey on the recording favorites *They're Either Too Young or Too Old* and *Besame Mucho* (it means *Kiss Me Much*), a duet with vocalist Bob Eberly, and, by the time she was 18, sparkled effortlessly under trumpet playing Harry James' tutelage with a cluster of #1 hits that became standards before she reached the age of twenty.

Do you remember who that was?

Well, sure, you say, that's easy!

It's pretty Katherine "Kitty" Kallen.

Okay! You're right!

But strangely enough, some people *need* to be reminded of Kitty Kallen's sensational performances with the Big Bands. She holds the distinction of being the only girl singer who was featured with four of the most famous Big Bands: Artie Shaw, Harry James, and both Dorseys—Tommy and Jimmy. Not that Jack Teagarden's band was a lightweight; that would make it five. People seem to be more familiar with those very popular singles Kitty originated beyond the Big Band days: those terrific hits *Little Things Mean a Lot* (that lovely song suited her perfectly) and *In the Chapel in the Moonlight* in 1954; *If I Give My Heart to You* in 1959, and the immensely popular RCA recording *My Coloring Book* in 1962 that again won her the acclaim she richly deserved.

55

Although blockbusters all, I personally prefer those early Big Band gems and the rhythmically advanced swinging style she delivered during her tenure with the those bands. For me, maybe it's simply a matter of time-frame and musical choices.

While trying to organize this book, the sequel to *The Best Damn Trumpet Player,* one of the most elusive subjects to locate was this underrated, expressive vocalist Kitty Kallen, the former teen-age girl vocalist from Philadelphia. She had moved out of the California star umbrella and relocated to a charming home on the east coast, believing it was a more genuine atmosphere for living where people were *real* and didn't automatically recite their resume' every time they ran into you at an airport or restaurant.

If you want to talk to Kitty Kallen during the winter, you'll have to wait until she returns from her six-months-a-year hangout in Mexico (she adores the Indian culture as well as the climate), her most favorite place other than her permanent Hudson River-style home in Northern New Jersey.

Recently Kitty co-hosted a two-hour Harry James tribute on New Jersey radio station WVNJ -AM. The show, *In The Spotlight,* is hosted by my friend, ex-WNEW, New York newsman Mike Prelee, whose daily newscasts for many years preceded William B. Williams' legendary *Make Believe Ballroom* segments. The program became an inadvertent showcase for Kitty Kallen where she revealed some interesting secrets about herself and her ex-boss, bandleader Harry James, who hired her immediately after Helen Forrest left the band.

While talking with Kitty at her New Jersey home in a beautifully decorated room with a magnificent grand piano, she admitted being nervous when first replacing Helen, "There I was, following another Helen. First it was Helen O'Connell who I followed in Jimmy Dorsey's band, and now Helen Forrest in Harry James' band. Well, I mentioned to Harry that I was a little bit nervous, but he managed to make me feel so comfortable I soon forgot my butterflies. He told me not to worry, that I'd do just fine, and....I did!"

Kitty got along extremely well with Harry James: "Harry was a very good teacher and a great boss. I had the honor of working with him every single night. He was the most talented musician I ever worked with. He was gifted and modest. Harry loved what he was doing, and you knew when you were on the bandstand that he liked what you were doing. You didn't have to prove anything to Harry. He appreciated your work. And I never, ever heard Harry rehearse or warm up for a show," she went on to say, "Jack Teagarden and Jimmy Dorsey always practiced scales to warm up for a show; Harry never did that. Don't you think that was amazing? And he never talked shop in the off hours. It was one of the greatest periods of my life."

On the Astor roof, May 22, 1943, the first year after she joined up, Kitty Kallen sang her first song with Harry James. It turned out to be one of the Swing Era's definitive jazz standards, *I'm Beginning to See the Light*. Gunther Schuller, author of the acclaimed chronicle *The Swing Era*, punctuated and praised this part band, part strings performance of Harry James and annotated it as *sung very well by Kitty Kallen*, an important compliment, for sure.

That long-standing evergreen was followed by the bouncy *Waiting for the Train to Come In* and the great wartime hit—*Kiss me once and kiss me twice, and kiss me once again...... It's Been a Long, Long Time*. How I love her rendition of that wonderful tune. Notably, *I'll Buy That Dream*, *I Guess I'll Hang Out My Tears to Dry,* and the still-popular *Candy* paraded right behind while she sung her heart out with the Harry James' band.

"Working for the Big Bands was a matter of discipline and hard work," Kitty ardently explained over a cup of tea, "You'd receive a song sheet in the morning and had to learn it and then perform it that very same evening. You rehearsed it all day until you got it right. The song *11:60 P.M.* was the toughest song I ever sang. I think I do 16 bars before taking a breath. The guys in the band would take bets. 'Is she going to take a breath, or isn't she?'

"I didn't enjoy singing that song, even though Harry wrote it. Now that most of these songs have been re-issued on digital CD's, the quality is unbelievable. When I hear it, no kidding, I feel like I am back sitting on the bandstand." Kitty was saying, "and I have a confession to make. I really never listened to myself. But, after listening to these new re-recordings, I think I was not too bad." Kitty has that rare vocal quality that wills you to listen to the words of a song, a straightforward purity of melody.

Kitty always enjoyed watching couples dance cheek-to-cheek as the band played while she sat out an instrumental—maybe *Chirichiribin* or any Big Band extra—"I was a little jealous—watching them snuggle up to one another—I think, I hope that kind of dancing is happening again."

Kitty left Harry James' band at the suggestion of James, who envisioned the inevitable industry change whereupon vocalists would become more important properties than the bands themselves, inadvertently forecasting the era of the great vocalists which, in retrospect, evolved as the bands gradually disbanded. "He said to me, 'Listen, Sinatra's out there; Peggy Lee and Perry Como are out there. They're all out there, and I think you are ready.' Then he added, 'Try it'. And I did. He was right!"

Kitty was one of the most sought after supper club singers when she first met publicist Budd Granoff in 1947 at the Copacabana Nightclub in New York City. They were married one year later. At the time, Buddy was press agent for a number of well-known performers, among them Frank Sinatra, Dean Martin & Jerry Lewis, Doris Day, and Jo Stafford. He quit the public relations business to manage Kitty's career.

Budd chose all Kitty's songs, including 1954's biggest hit record, #1 on the charts for an impressive twenty-six weeks, *Little Things Mean a Lot*. It was the kind of recording, Kay Starr said to me a few years ago, "that gets the memories starting" every time it is played.

But, then, you won't believe it—Kitty Kallen actually lost her voice along the otherwise smooth road.

Three long frightening years later, with help from husband Buddy and recording Artists & Repertoire man Mitch Miller, Kitty bravely broke what seemed like a curse to her. In 1959 she recorded *If I Give My Heart to You* and was back on the road to success. *That Old Feeling* and another Kitty Kallen favorite, *My Coloring Book*, followed right behind. *My Coloring Book* has been recorded by many artists since, but Kitty clearly "owns" it as sure as Kay Starr "owns" *Wheel of Fortune* and Rosemary Clooney "owns" *Tenderly*. Just think about those amazing blockbusters. And they sound just as fresh today. You somehow never tire of them.

Why, just today, Frankie Laine and I were talking about Kitty and Buddy, Frank saying that the very well-liked Buddy Granoff managed every facet of Kitty's career and was responsible for producing her albums and helping to catapult her into one of the leading Song Stars of the 1950's. But, it's also fair to say Kitty's own inner-sense of what's musically right for her contributed to that phenomenal post-band solo career. Jack Teagarden once advised Kitty: "...when you sing, just tell the story." Kitty put that advice into the proper perspective, along with a delicate sense of timing and a great deal of affection.

Ironically, once again at the top of her profession, Kitty learned she had developed blood spots on her lungs as a result of a wrongly administered prescription, forcing her into retirement. She simply was unable to sing a note. Now you know the reason behind her annual migration to Mexico. The cold and dampness of northern winters aggravate her condition.

It's amazing to realize that Kitty sang with every band but Benny Goodman's. As mentioned, she recorded with Artie Shaw (*My Heart Belongs to Daddy* in 1946), both Jimmy & Tommy Dorsey, Teagarden, and James. But when you talk to anyone about her illustrious career, the instant response is, "Oh Yeah! I remember her. Didn't she sing that song *Little Things Mean a Lot*?"...then they reminisce, "*blow me a kiss from across the room....say I look nice when I'm not.*" Well, can you blame them? It happens to me the very same way, and I know better. If you pick up her new CD, *The Kitty Kallen Story*, you will get the entire picture of her career straight in your mind once and for all.

Kitty Kallen was married for over 48 years to Buddy, who was a music publisher and very successful television syndicator. Sadly, Budd Granoff passed away on April 28, 1996. The loss has hit Kitty, her only son Jonathan, a United Nations attorney, and her three grandchildren very hard.

I met the very amiable Budd just once, while he was producing the very first Martin & Lewis Muscular Dystrophy telethon on March 15, 1952. It took place at NBC's New York Studio 6B, which was borrowed for 24 hours from Milton Berle whose *Texaco Star Theater* televison show appeared live every Tuesday night. (For many years later, it was Johnny Carson's *Tonite Show* New York studio). I was a volunteer working for the show along with other NBC personnel.

Kitty and Budd were also early strong supporters of the Society of Singers that assists singers and other performers who find themselves in serious financial need. Budd, with others, raised much needed revenue for the Society by producing an album entitled *A Gift Of Music*. A chapter about the Society appears in this book.

Kitty admires her peers who still keep performing. She smiles and even hints at one day returning to the fray. "Look at Rosemary (Clooney), Kay Starr and Margaret Whiting at Rainbow & Stars! They can't wait to get on stage! Sinatra.....when he performed recently, it's like a religious experience.! It's great for them, but I don't really miss it. I'm happy at home with my family and friends and my charity work. They say I'm a living icon now, whatever that is. Maybe some day........" Kitty has performed recently in local charity events, one with Song Star Margaret Whiting.

And, as a special surprise gift, Kitty was able to obtain a great photo of her with Harry James for this book from Sony Music. The photo was produced on a Fujufilm 100MB zip drive disk and transferred from a computer to the hard copy on the face page of her chapter. Isn't that a great blend of nostalgia and hi-tech?

Little things mean a lot for Kitty Kallen these days. We promised to get together again this summer when *Song Stars* is published and she's back in her lovely New Jersey home.

Authors Note: Sony has just released Kitty's brand new album *Sweet With A Beat* featuring all her work with Harry James.

CONNIE HAINES

Recapture the Feeling

One spring evening, shortly after the June, 1996, release of the first book in this series, *The Best Damn Trumpet Player*, I sent a signed copy with a letter soliciting comments to former Big Band vocalist Connie Haines, now an international star in her own right, and promptly received an absolutely stunning hand-written reply in green ink by return mail. The shade of ink matched the logo, a simulated music staff header that headlined *Connie Haines Enterprises Inc* surrounded by a floating bevy of dancing eighth and quarter-notes. It read:

Dear Richard:

Thanks for this great book. Reading about all my good friends and my best friend, Helen O'Connell, made me very happy. But, I'm so disappointed you did not interview me too, since I have so many personal memories of Satchmo and Harry James as we worked together throughout the years.

But, God is Good—I've continued to have a full-time career and I recorded my best album in 1988, that is still selling well. Last November I performed for three weeks in a fabulous show saluting the end of World War II, saluting the USO and all my work with Bing Crosby, Bob Hope, and Frank Sinatra at Trump's Taj Mahal in Atlantic City. My life's work was shown on dual screens during the 1 1/2 hour concert. I am flying all over the country for various State Governors with this inspiring show.

Then I'm sailing for Russia on a cruise tour. It's all so exciting. C'mon let's get another book going. Richard, get back to me.

God Bless, Connie.

Connie Haines with Tommy Dorsey 1939. (Connie Haines Collection)

Reacting to that encouraging note, I contacted my friend Don Kennedy, host of Atlanta's Big Band Jump syndicated radio, who promptly arranged a telephone interview with Connie for a career update for the July-August, 1996 Newsletter that makes its way every two months into the homes of thousands of Big Band *aficionados*. The newsletter did a great job promoting *Trumpet Player*, and Connie was also trying to promote her original book, *For Once in My Life* (which is, also, her favorite and most recorded song), to fans with all proceeds going to the non-profit Connie Haines Living Center and Cancer Foundation. Connie was pleased, always happy to report the uplifting news of her life to the faithful and gather funds for her Foundation. And then I spoke to Connie about a new idea for another book to be entitled *The Song Stars*, the title a suggestion from a photo in her own book on page 231 where a Strand Theater marquee' reads, "Connie Haines, Radio's loveliest *song star*," on a co-bill with another upcoming singer, a guy named Perry Como.

But, wait a minute—hold on. We are getting ahead of things. Let's drift back a few decades into one of America's old southern cities, Savannah, Georgia, where a beautiful baby, Yvonne Marie JaMais, was born to aristocratic parents. Known since for most of her life as Connie Haines, a sobriquet assigned to her by ex-boss Harry James when she was only 15, Yvonne always *knew* she one day would be a famous singer.

Characteristically, from very early in her life, Connie Haines always begins each day with a prayer,

Father God,
I place my hand in Yours today.
Here is my life. Show me the way.

Her first public appearance was at age four in the *Baby Saucy Show in* Savannah, and at five she was already Florida state Charleston champion. After rapid success in those formative years, dancing and singing reached deep into her blood. She loved to perform. Aunts and uncles enthusiastically encouraged her, and her loving mother moved her carefully along. It was the jazz age of Al Jolson, Sophie Tucker, Ed Wynn, and Eddie Cantor. Then success at an amateur contest led to an NBC contract as the *Little Princess of the Air* which lasted for a year. Later, after a bout with scarlet fever, Connie began singing in Miami, Florida, as a vocalist with Howard Lally's orchestra. When auditioning for representation by the William Morris Agency, in the old Brill Building in New York City, band leader Harry James happened to be present and heard Connie sing *I Cried For You* and *I Can't Give You Anything But Love, Baby*. He called some two hours later and offered the sixteen year old a job with the band. She started that very night at forty dollars a week, opening at the old Benjamin Franklin Hotel in Philadelphia. "I remember I wore a white taffeta gown," Connie said.

"Yvonne Marie Antoinette JaMais is quite a name, but it won't fit on the marquee'," Harry James considered carefully, "No, you look like a *Connie* to me. Haines! Connie Haines! It goes with James." He was quite sure, and the young lady nodded *okay*. Listening to the radio expecting to hear her daughter Yvonne sing with the James band, her mother almost called the police until she heard her voice and realized the singer introduced as Connie Haines was, in fact, her own little Yvonne Marie.

"We went on the road in a band bus. After several nights of sleeping on a bus, it was a strange feeling to check into a Main Street hotel; be able to hang up your clothes; to wash your hands when you wanted to, not when the bus driver told you to; and to lie on a bed that wasn't moving in a normal sleeping position. But it was an exhilarating experience. Then a wonderful guy named Frank Sinatra joined us."

Harry James tried to change Frank Sinatra's name too, but, according to Connie, a confident Frank said typically: "You want the voice, you take the name."

"Frank was lots of fun on the bus trips. He was always in good spirits. He pitched in, always doing his share and more," Connie confided. The recording Connie made with Harry, *Comes Love, Nothing Can Be Done*, is my absolute Connie Haines favorite. She sounds so young, so cute, so bubbly, energetic and charming. I also favor *Don't Worry 'Bout Me*, typically pleasant Haines material to listen to over and over.

"You know, Richard, I don't *sound* that way anymore. That was *fifty* years ago. I made that record singing to cold padded walls. A microphone was stuck in my face. All I could feel was panic. But it became a hit record. It was not until I joined Tommy Dorsey months later that I finally began to feel relaxed when recording. I really love my audiences. They are my friends. I prefer singing to them live."

Frank and Connie eventually joined Tommy Dorsey's band, as James' organization was faltering financially at the time. He eventually came back into the fray, however, after the success of *You Made Me Love You*, a song Harry greatly admired after hearing a very young Judy Garland sing her heart out to a Clark Gable photo in a sentimental MGM movie, and after heavy promotion by Martin Block on the New York radio station WNEW on his show, the original *Make Believe Ballroom*. Connie's version of that tune became a hit for her later on.

"Frank and I developed a little feud when we were with Dorsey," Connie revealed to me, "and he would not sing at the same mike with me. He would not even look at me. So I would pick a young man or two in the front row," she continued, "and direct my singing at him on songs like *Snooty Little Cutie*, or *Oh! Look at Me Now*, or *Let's Get Away from It All*, and that would make Frank even madder. But we finally stopped teasing one another, then kissed and made up on New Year's eve night in 1941.

On those recordings, Connie said, she would get ten dollars and Frank twenty-five, even though they sold millions of records. "That's the agreement we had. We were unknown kids and he (Tommy Dorsey) was training us." Dorsey's was considered the star-maker band.

Connie was so young with Dorsey that to do one-nighters her mother had to give Dorsey guardianship, accomplished before a judge in order for her to travel interstate on a bus with all those men in the band.

Tommy Dorsey also featured The Pied Pipers, a singing group (currently owned and managed by my friend, trombonist Warren Covington, who succeeded Tommy Dorsey) comprised of three young men and beautiful Jo Stafford. They performed immortal songs like *I'll Never Smile Again* and others backing up Connie and Frank. *What*

Is This Thing Called Love and *Will You Still Be Mine* were hits for Connie, the latter written especially for her by Matt Dennis and Tom Adaire. Her favorite Sinatra duets remain *Oh! Look at Me Now* and *Let's Get Away from It All*, arranged by Sy Oliver. "I use those arrangements right to this day. The audience just loves it."

Connie admits being influenced by Billie Holiday, Mildred Bailey, and Kate Smith. While convalescing with childhood rheumatic fever, she studiously observed the sound of Kate Smith on the radio, always desiring to emulate those powerful phrases, continuing it right up to today.

Connie told me the famous story of how her dress once caught fire back stage while performing with Tommy Dorsey at New York's old Madison Square Garden: "While I was backstage getting ready to sing, someone threw a cigarette from one of the tier seats. It caught in my net dress and ignited. I was enveloped in flames. Frank Sinatra threw his jacket off and slammed it at me. It knocked me to the floor. I did not know what hit me. The coat and the fall snuffed out the flames. My long hair was scorched and the back of my dress was burned off. Tommy kept vamping while I was on fire. He wasn't aware of what was happening. Back up on my feet, I heard my cue and ran on stage. I moved up to the mike and let go right on the beat."

Tommy's mouth dropped when he realized what had happened as they noticed the burnt dress with the sides flying. Connie feels that her early rooted, life-long training enabled her to go on with the show.

"In those days, I considered myself a stylist," Connie said, "when it was more important than possessing a great big voice, like Kate Smith's. The record-makers were looking for that individual, special sound." Connie sings quite differently today letting go with all her volume and rhythm. In those days she sang with a distinct beat in her voice. Where most girl vocalists sang smooth, she was said to swing. "Helen O'Connell was a great stylist. Helen Forrest was a ballad singer with a clear, pure voice," she added, "Kitty (Kallen), was personality plus. Peggy Lee was the most sensuous."

The Tommy Dorsey band tour wound up in Hollywood. Their first movie for MGM, *Ship Ahoy*, also starred dancer Eleanor Powell.

But, exhausted by the long tour, Connie elected to quit the band but remained in Hollywood for four years as the Song Star of the *Abbott and Costello Radio Show,* performing in theaters from coast to coast during the summer hiatus.

Connie soon became the star of an easy, half-hour variety radio show, *Your Blind Date*, involving servicemen audience participation and listeners as well. It was Hollywood's answer to New York's *Stage Door Canteen.*

At that time, songwriter Johnny Mercer formed a new record company called Capitol, and Connie cut a record *He Wears a Pair of Silver Wings,* conducted by Gordon Jenkins. It was her first solo recording after her band associations. She soon became a cover girl, gracing *Variety, Billboard, Downbeat*, and *Life* magazines.

Connie subsequently made movies at MGM. There was The *Duchess of Idaho* with Van Johnson & Esther Williams and ten additional films. She recorded countless sides, played in night spots, and even made guest appearances on Bob Hope's and Bing Crosby's radio shows. She sang in the Billy Graham *Youth For Christ* movement, too. She was clearly in her element—expression in entertainment and dedication and personal involvement in what she believed. Real fun was church participation and singing to our servicemen.

Later, she starred in summer stock production as Anita in *West Side Story*, in *Showboat* and *Come Blow Your Horn*, and then with Mickey Rooney, replacing an ailing Judy Garland on a national theater tour. "Judy was the greatest talent of all time, to step into her shoes and take her place on stage, I would've gladly sung without being paid," she acknowledged.

"I had my own television show for years with Frankie Laine, all throughout the fifties, and then we traveled for years all over the country performing in theaters everywhere as Mister and Miss Rhythm," Connie proudly said. She loves Frankie Laine.

Over the years Connie has appeared with so many stars and on so many shows that it would be impossible to list them all in this chronicle. But meritorious to mention are performances with jazz pioneer Louis Armstrong and no less than five command performances for four Presidents: Eisenhower, Kennedy, Johnson, and Ronald Reagan

Connie Haines today.
(Richard Grudens Collection)

(twice). It was at the 50th anniversary of Pearl Harbor when she appeared with President Bush.

Her best friends today are those with whom she shares her life-long religious life. Actress Rhonda Fleming, British singer Beryl Davis, actress and vocalist Jane Russell. "We teamed up singing gospel songs in 1954 for Decca Records. Our first recording *Do Lord* was a million seller. There were twenty-six other hits we sang while touring half-way round the world in concert until 1984. We grew up together in the church; we got married all at the same time and had wedding showers and prayed for babies....and now we've got 'umpteen grandkids." She sometimes flies out to the coast from her Florida home to do one-nighters just to see her friends.

In 1982 Connie had a radical bi-lateral mastectomy and had to have three years of chemo-therapy: "But I can honestly say that I never got sick, never lost my hair and I never missed a show on the road. It was not only my own personal faith in God, but belief in the attitude-health connection and the power of the mind that can heal the body, and here I am fourteen years later."

Connie received the Courage Award in 1988 from President Ronald Reagan at a White House ceremony for the American Cancer Society.

"I've had quite a life. I'm a full-time minister and I've got a son and a daughter and three grandkids and a 98 year old mother I took out just yesterday afternoon, and I'm busy, busy, busy." Connie does lots of cruise "gigs" these days: "It's a paid vacation. You go out on a trip and you don't have to pay for it. Quality is the word with stretch limos, first-class transportation on planes, and the presidential suite on the ships. That's pretty nice, I'd say."

Connie's main mission today is to tell her story about beating cancer, imparting inspiration to those around her, influencing others to pursue treatment where many of them were reluctant to seek medical assistance. "I'm living proof that you can be victorious over that disease," she insists.

I'm so happy about my association with Connie Haines. I'm sorry we did not get together much earlier. She has lived nine lives for sure (I think with my intervention, probing her life's work and times while also soliciting some of her priceless photographs for this book, we can add a *tenth*). You can find out more about that in her autobiography mentioned earlier. When I want to enjoy Connie's company, I simply select any of her recordings any time I wish and she appears, serving up those enchanting songs just for me.

On October 1, 1996, Connie called me after spending three weeks in the hospital for, as she says, "a bunch of problems," and to recount her recent appearance in Atlanta, Georgia, her home state, where she was received by the Governor and countless fans—more than she could believe.

"They shouted out to me, and it made me feel no pain," she announced with her usual, uplifting spirit. Connie Haines loves her fans, and her fans love Connie Haines.

In early December, Connie returned to the hospital to wrap up the balance of her problems. "When I get out," she promised, "I will write you a *foreword* for *Song Stars*."

"Sure!" I returned, "You'll have to stay home for six weeks...no traveling...no performing....I've got you grounded." (But I was thrilled—see the foreword.) "And," she added, "I'll find some time to locate those photos of Louis Armstrong and myself...and also the photos with Jane (Russell) and Beryl (Davis) for the book."

"That would be great!" replied grateful me.

Connie Haines is always in demand, even today. With a strong following of listeners on KORK radio in Las Vegas, she'll have to return there soon to satisfy the faithful. She worked last July, August and September, like a teenage trouper, covering the Florida circuit. For her, hospital stays become "vacations," or days off.

Connie's fans really keep her going strong. Her friends keep her even stronger.

"*Comes love,*" she added, "*nothing can be done.*"

Connie Haines and Ella Fitzgerald share a smile.
(Connie Haines Collection)

Doris Day sings at NBC Studios, Hollywood 1955.
(Don Kennedy Collection)

DORIS DAY

Little Miss Kappelhoff from Cincinnati

One hot summer day in 1948, when I was sixteen and living in Brooklyn, New York, I ducked into my air-conditioned neighborhood movie theater to seek relief from the rising temperature and to see *Romance on the High Seas*. In the cool darkness, a young band singer turned actress vocalized the movie's romantic ballad *It's Magic*. I became enamored by both song and song star, pretty and fresh-looking Doris Day, the post-war girl next door. The song's lucid structure and her slow, natural delivery ushered in a new groundbreaking for female singers. I remained for three showings. It was a *magical* afternoon.

Retracing eight years earlier: While Benny Goodman was re-organizing his old band and Lionel Hampton was starting a new band, this young seventeen year-old ex-dancer from Cincinnati, formerly Doris Kappelhoff, whose idols were Betty Grable and Ginger Rogers, began a band singing career with the little-known Barney Rapp Band in Cincinnati. He promptly switched her name to Doris Day, having once heard her singing *Day After Day* on a local amateur radio hour.

"I thought *Doris Day* sounded so phony!" said Doris, "He said he thought it sounded just perfect, and my mother liked it; I really never did. It didn't sound real. Isn't that funny?"

Doris had turned to singing after her dancing career was sidelined by a shattered leg incurred in an auto-train accident. "To encourage me in music, the doctor gave me a ukulele, but it didn't mean much. When I was dancing I, also, sang in a personality class. We would pick a song that we liked and sing a chorus and then we would make up a dance to perform in front of the other kids." Doris said that her father had a wonderful voice, "He had perfect pitch. He taught piano, violin, and theory and even directed a choir."

73

Ella Fitzgerald was a definite influence in Doris' life: "The one voice I listened to above others belonged to Ella Fitzgerald. Her voice fascinated me, so I'd sing along with her, trying to catch the subtle way she sang the words."

One of Doris' early Big Band affiliations was with Bing's brother Bob Crosby. One evening in 1986, while I was on a Bob Hope interview backstage at Westbury Music Fair, Les Brown told me he first went to see Doris while she was performing with Crosby at the Edison Hotel in New York. In his famous boyish manner, he offered her a job and signed her up, "Like many others at that time, she was unhappy in the Crosby organization, so she readily accepted. I simply asked her if she wanted to join up with my band. As a result of their dissatisfaction Bob Crosby lost some pretty good arrangers too, like Ray Coniff, Henry Mancini, Nelson Riddle and Paul Weston."

"I was so happy to join up with Les, isn't that funny? He just had to ask me. But I stayed for only one year," Doris told Big Band Broadcast host Chris Valenti of Long Island's WHPC FM radio who interviewed Doris last week.

"I ran a tight ship," Les said, "The band was clean with no drinking, drugs or hard language while working. Doris' first recording was the ditty *Beau Night in Hotchkiss Corners*. Doris was so young that her mother enlisted the help of my trusted trombonist, Si Zentner, who took her to work and brought her home very night."

"I was very lucky working with Les," Doris said. "The boys were so great. They softened things up for me when everything could have disillusioned and soured me." The Les Brown Band Of Renown became known inside the business as "The Milkshake Band." "And," according to Les, "If ever there was a milk-shake girl, it was Doris."

"Then I left the band to get married and Lester was furious. He was so mad. And it turned out to be a terrible mistake," Doris said. "So I took a job in Cinncinnati at WLW, a really huge station. My old singing coach knew the manager and got me a job on a show called *Moon River* at midnight, for goodness sake. I sang three love songs each night. One night Les and the boys heard me in their rented car—they were on tour and were traveling through the area. Les said...'Hey, that's Dodo singing. We've got to get her back in the band'. They found where I lived and haunted me until I agreed to go back. But I had my son, Terry, but my mother agreed to travel with us and help take care of him. And that's how it happened! I went back with Lester." Les is now eighty-five and, by his own recent admission, is still a band leader and is listed in the *Guiness Book of Records* accordingly.

The more memorable *My Dreams are Getting Better all the Time* and Doris' biggest big-band hit, *Sentimental Journey* which consistently appears on the Top Ten all-time list of songs of that era when polls are re-taken, were recorded in 1944 after she re-joined the band.

"Nobody was especially impressed when we first played that tune," Doris recalled, "But after we played it on a couple of broadcasts, the mail started pouring in. Before that I don't think we'd even planned to record it. But of course we did-right away—and you know the rest."

"We had so much fun in our band bus when we were on tour. The guys were so funny," Doris revealed, "We just laughed all the time. We were a family. We laughed and we cried—I'll always have those memories. I love Lester and wish he could come up to Carmel and visit me."

Doris left the Les Brown band again in 1946 and worked the night club circuit for a while, including dueting a couple of winsome recordings in 1947 with soft-crooner Buddy Clark: *Love Somebody* and *Confess*. And how about their version of *Baby It's Cold Outside.*

Down on her luck, having a tough time trying to make ends meet while living in a trailer in Hollywood and supporting her new baby, she was helped by Mannie Sachs, a well-liked NBC vice-president (I later worked under Mannie myself a few years later), who helped arrange a night club job for Doris. She landed a contract at the Little Club in New York even though it lasted only a few months. She was soon back in Hollywood trying to rearrange her life.

Doris' start in the movies was accidental: "Acting in films had never so much as crossed my mind. I was a singer and all my talents were motivated toward that," she said.

Fortunately, and unbeknowned to Doris, movie director Michael Curtiz was frantically searching for a lead actress/singer for a musical that was ready for filming, *Romance on the High Seas.* The score, including the song *It's Magic*, written by Sammy Cahn and Jule Styne for Judy Garland whose deal with the studio fell through, was just perfect for Doris' style and personality. The songwriters were able to convince Doris to sing at a party at Jule Styne's house:

"Jule told me he and Sammy just wrote a score for a movie and wanted to know if I was interested in playing the leading role. I gasped and said that I thought they would want an experienced singer and Sammy said, 'I'm not so sure.' " This led to a screen test the next morning. The test was frenetic and hectic, but Doris wound up with the part. As Curtiz said in his thick Hungarian accent, "I sometimes like girl who is not actress. Is less pretend and more heart." *It's Magic* became a #1 top seller for months.

In between films with Warner, Doris did travel with Bob Hope's USO troupe in 1948. "Doris is one of the great singers," said Bob during our last interview, "she really puts over a song. She has a good sense of timing, like Bing Crosby. She is one of my favorites. She has that quality that lights up the house. When she sings a ballad, she can really get to you."

While with Warner Brothers she appeared in a series of mostly minor backstage type musicals with various co-stars—Ronald Reagan, Gene Nelson, Jack Carson, Gordon MacRae, and Gene Kelly. It was with Kirk Douglas (her voice juxtaposing Harry James' expressive trumpet) where I feel she touchdowned a significant mark in her singing and film career in the 1949 *Young Man with a Horn,* a movie based on the life of legendary jazz cornetist Bix Beiderbecke. It was so well done. It produced an abundant album of great songs with *With a Song in My Heart* lighting the way and Harry James' crying trumpet playing background and release. In 1952, a film *I'll See You in My Dreams* with Danny Thomas, about song lyricist Gus Kahn, was also a high musical spot in Doris' film career. I just got a copy of that black and white film today. It was the Doris Day I loved. Simple, young and pretty, an ingenue. Danny Thomas' back-up was perfect.

Doris recorded the bouncy *A Guy Is a Guy* that year and, with my friend Frankie Laine, a South African duet called *Sugarbush*. In 1953 she captured "gold" with her big hit film, the rambunctious, two-fisted *Calamity Jane* co-starring he-man-singer Howard Keel. She served up the exhilarating songs *The Deadwood Stage* and her 1954 Oscar

**Doris Day on the set of *The Man Who Knew Too Much*
with Alfred Hitchcock.
(Richard Grudens Collection)**

winning ballad, *Secret Love*. The film *Young at Heart* in 1955 with her earlier radio show *Hit Parade* partner, Frank Sinatra, and *I'll Never Stop Loving You,* from the film *Love Me or Leave Me,* a chronicle of earlier vocalist Ruth Etting, with Jimmy Cagney gave her worthy dramatic opportunities. *Que Sera, Sera (Whatever will be, will be)*, which aptly describes Doris' personal attitude toward life, sparkled as an Oscar winning song from the movie *The Man Who Knew Too Much*, filmed mostly in Marrakesh and London, directed by Alfred Hitchcock and co-starring Jimmy Stewart. "I just never expected that song to become a hit," Doris said. It is the song best identified with Doris by later fans just as *Sentimental Journey* is the favorite with earlier admirers.

"Wow, what an experience making that movie was," she further explained. "It was bizarre. In Marrakesh it was over 100 degrees every day and you roasted. Then in London it was freezing, so I caught pleurisy and had to stay in bed for a week. The traveling was difficult. But Jimmy Stewart is my darling friend and I appreciated appearing with him and working for Alfred."

The Pajama Game in 1957 with Broadway tenor John Raitt was probably her best musical endeavor and a big commercial hit for the studio. Her last musical film, *Jumbo,* in 1962 did not fare as well, but that is subjective. Doris' last top forty hit recording was *Everybody Loves A Lover*.

Doris' movie career covered 20 years and 39 films—lasting until 1968. Of course, the popular comedies *Pillow Talk* with Rock Hudson, *That Touch of Mink* with Cary Grant, *Teacher's Pet* with Clark Gable, *Please Don't Eat the Daisies* with David Niven, and *It Happened to Jane* with Jack Lemmon are fondly remembered by Doris Day movie fans.

There have been some dark days in the life of Doris Day, including several early brief marriages and later, serious financial problems. Upon her husband Marty Melcher's passing, it was discovered her life savings had been grossly mishandled, depriving her of all her money and assets. This unfortunate condition left Doris in serious debt which took years to resolve.

During the period of 1968 to 1972 it was *The Doris Day Show* on television. At first Doris reluctantly honored contracts set up by her late husband. The show started off with scripts and venues. Eventually she turned the show around, hiring new producers and scriptwriters who worked out a new format, somewhat emulating the comedy movies accomplished with Rock Hudson, like *Pillow Talk.*

Thanks to her earlier faith in the Christian Science Church, Doris has retained revelations. Not calling herself anything special or attaching herself to any organized church, her own personal expressions can be revealed in her own words: "Our body is the temple of the living God. We place our body at God's disposal to use as He chooses. Thus our body becomes an instrument for God, with the 'I' as the center of our being. There is no age or youth in the body. No strength or weakness in it. The body is an instrument for the 'I,' The God within us. Instead of praying up to God, we should instead be so silent with ourselves that we can hear the still small voice. That is when God manifests and expresses himself. Which is the creative and maintaining principle of our being. That is the essence of my metaphysical belief. That is my own personal religion."

Today, Doris still receives many scripts from hopeful producers. "...but I haven't really found one I'd just jump for joy to do, and so I'm not going to do something just to be busy. If I work, I love it; if I don't work, I love it. I never fret that I'm not working. I'm very busy here with my animals I love and adore, and I have this great home in the choice spot in Carmel."

Doris Day's life thrives on eleven acres in lush Carmel, California, where she keeps all her "babies." Those "babies" are all her pets. "My life is so full—thanks to all my beautiful pets," she says. Her motto is "Thanks for Caring" a message from her Doris Day Animal League, a non-profit organization dedicated to aiding abused animals. One of its priorities is to stop the needless suffering of animals used in testing. "It's the four-leggers that make everything work, make everything worthwhile and everything beautiful," she added.

In 1975 her full and detailed life story was written by A.E. Hotchner, entitled *Doris Day: Her Own Story.* It is a refreshing and uplifting story, compelling and honest almost to a fault:

"...my public image of America's la-di-da happy-go-lucky virgin, carefree and brimming with happiness was more make-believe than any part I ever played in any movie. Doris Day, a woman I know well, is the real subject of this book. This is the life I lived."

When I last heard from Doris, it was a letter of thanks for an advance copy of *The Best Damn Trumpet Player*. Because she was so busy with her animals, Doris was just opening her Christmas mail (this was now April, 1996). Tracing Doris' story is surely an amazing one. "I live now," she said when I asked about her future, "I don't live in the future. I don't live in the past, I live right now. Right now everything is just lovely." She told me she really means it!

Besides my lifelong enjoyment of Doris Day's songs and movies, she let me in on one of her health secrets: "....get one of those stationary bikes that you can ride in the house. There is no better instant tonic than to jump on it and pedal away for ten minutes." Best advice I ever had, especially pedaling while listening to Doris Day records.

HELEN O'CONNELL

Every Singer's Friend

In the early 1950's I went to work for NBC News in New York and wound up gathering news for *The Today Show*. In 1956 Big Band singer Helen O'Connell joined that same, now classic, morning show as co-host to the show's pioneer host, Dave Garroway. That's the one entity Helen and I held in common until our paths crossed head-on one evening in 1984. This time, Helen, backstage in a crisp between-shows housecoat, stood replying to trivial questions I pursued about her still lively career, while I held a tape-recorder in one hand and a group of 3 x 5 cards in the other. We finally found ourselves face-to-face with music the only common denominator.

"I guess the high point of my musical career was when Bob Eberly and I sang those great duets for Jimmy Dorsey," she said with that famous, cute, mischievous grin, while sipping some hot tea. "People loved those recordings...and they still ask me about them."

Standing on the sidelines at this meeting held in an anteroom to her Westbury Music Fair dressing room, friend and fellow performer Frankie Laine joined the conversation reminding Helen and I that it was during a chance breakfast meeting with Jimmy Dorsey's secretary, Nita Moore, on a New York Street that Frank learned from Nita about Jimmy's search for a girl singer.

"It happened that I saw Helen the night before at the Village Barn down on Eighth Street (he takes Helen's hand in his —) singing with Larry Funk and his band, so I told Nita about her and Jimmy went to see her perform and that's how he hired her," he recalled, glancing at Helen who was nodding her head up and down in approval.

81

Richard Grudens shares a smile with Helen O'Connell. (Photo C. Camille Smith)

"It couldn't have happened better for me. That was the beginning of my being known at all. That was my favorite band and Bob Eberly was my favorite singer, but," she leans over and plants a smooch on Frank's bearded cheek, "I *love* Frank, too!"

At the beginning of Helen's career, an issue of *Downbeat Magazine* called her a cross between Ella Fitzgerald and Mildred Bailey, a really odd combination for sure. Bob Eberly once told me in a telephone conversation that Helen squeaked her voice cutely on the recording of *Green Eyes* when she sang, and emphasized the phrase "those cute and limpid, green eyes" because "she just couldn't reach the high notes," implying a limited vocal range. Helen denied it completely: ".....it was just my preferred way of accenting the phrase." The popularity of those duet recordings earned her top spot in the *Metronome* poll of 1940.

Helen O'Connell came to light on May 23, 1920, in Lima, Ohio. She first sang by the very delicate age of 13. "My father died and I had to help support our family, so I left home at sixteen," she recalled, "but I did sing professionally when I was thirteen with the Austin Wylie Orchestra back in Cleveland."

Helen considers the *second* recording she ever made, *All of Me*, her favorite, "...and I also think George Gershwin's *Embraceable You* was one of my best, too." They both define her singing skills quite clearly.

"What about, *Jim*? I asked, referring to her hit single *Jim Never Sends Me Pretty Flowers*.

"Oh, yeah, I know. I guess I love that one, too!" Lots of people do too!

It's amazing how Helen hadn't changed much from the 1950's to the 1980's. She retained that perky, youthful appearance throughout the industrious, grueling years of the Big Band Era right up to now: "We'd work all day in a theater sometimes doing five shows, then we'd go to someplace like the Cafe' Rouge (a nightclub in New York's Hotel Pennsylvania) and do a few more shows. I was lucky if I ever saw another girl singer that I knew or a musician somewhere along the line, unless we went to 52nd Street (the New York City jazz nightclubs center of the time) for a rare night out. We were all very busy and the years passed quickly, and here we are."

It's curious that Helen O'Connell is perhaps the best-known singer and one of the best-loved performers of the Big Band Era, probably because of the recordings *Green Eyes* and *Tangerine* alone. It's curious to note that that group of famous duets, including *Amapola* and *Yours,* were created quite accidentally: The Jimmy Dorsey Orchestra was allotted just three minutes at the close of a formatted weekly radio show, so arranger Tutti Camaratta devised a unique formula that featured all the stars of the series. Bob Eberly sang the first chorus of a song as a ballad, then the tempo was to pick up so the entire band would play part of the selection, then the tempo was to slow down and Helen came in for a semi-wailing finale. The formula worked so well that Dorsey used it on subsequent recordings, and *Green Eyes* alone sold 90,000 copies in a few days, which was a record in a time when 25,000 copies was equal to a million seller today.

After doing three movies with Jimmy Dorsey, they offered Helen a movie contract. She was to do a Bing Crosby, Fred Astaire picture (probably *Blue Skies* or *Holiday Inn*). When they realized she could not and would not dance, it ended before it began. Of course, Helen had actually taught dancing at one time, but she was more interested at this time in getting married and bringing up a family than in the fame and fortune earned through making movies. She did marry and had four girls with first husband Cliff Smith.

"Later, when I went back to work I had more offers to do movies, but I began working with Frank De Vol at the Palladium and then went on the road with singer Vic Damone for some very good money."

Further statistics reveal Helen as hostess for CBS's *Top Tunes* show in 1953; star of her own NBC show in the late fifties; interviewer for NBC's *Here's Hollywood,* and hostess for the *Miss Universe Pageant* for nine years. Fellow vocalists Margaret Whiting, Rosemary Clooney and Kay Starr toured with Helen for a spell in an act they called *Four Girls Four* that terminated when the girls apparently got on one-another's nerves and the length and effort of touring became tiring. Helen has appeared on and off with the orchestras of Woody Herman, Glenn Miller and Artie Shaw. Her

**L to R: Song Stars Connie Haines, Kitty Kallen and Helen O'Connell.
(Connie Haines Collection)**

commercials (she was once the spokesperson for Polaroid), personal appearances and recordings are too many to list.

In 1991, Helen and composer-conductor Frank DeVol tied the knot. As both active participant and board member Helen spent endless time with the Society of Singers, an L.A. based charitable association that assists down-and-out singers and other musical performers. She spent lots and lots of quality time with her grandchildren, too.

During 1992, Helen was kept pretty busy headlining eight Jimmy Dorsey concerts including some cruise ship adventures. An August, 1993, Big Band show at Valley Forge Music Fair in Pennsylvania, the sister showcase to Westbury Music Fair where we held our interview, was the last known professional performance of Helen O'Connell.

During an interview with the *Big Band Jump Newsletter*, Helen was once asked: "What question do people most often ask you?"

Among some other things this warm, caring, and lovable vocalist of the Big Band Era said: "People often ask me about the Big Band Era and all the other wonderful performers, but I can't answer that. I know I was continuously working. I tell the people, if I'd known the Big Band Era was going to be so important, I'd have paid more attention to it."

This accomplished lady may have been recognized for her great recordings, but again, loving babies were very much more important to her than a celebrity life in music. "My real kicks in life are just being around my little, tiny grandchildren," she said ever so warmly.

Why, in 1990 Helen even had a great-grandchild by the name of Gentry Allen! She enjoyed the remaining three precious years of her life with those beloved babes. Fortunately for us, the music featuring Helen O'Connell goes on through her evergreen recordings. Her philosophy about the art of singing summed up like this:

"Those who are successful don't need any advice from me. Those who are just starting out must be willing to pay their dues. I don't mean work for peanuts—get all you can, but don't turn your nose up at getting learning experience. Sing whenever you can. You just have to keep trying until somebody (important in show business) hears you and hands you a break, a start. I think you have to know something about your trade once you get there."

Helen O'Connell lost her battle with cancer in 1993.

Peggy Lee 1942. Note inscription to Jack Ellsworth.
(Jack Ellsworth Collection)

PEGGY LEE

A Lyrics Drama

"Well, I've never been able to define a jazz singer," Peggy Lee said, "but I can tell when I hear one." Then she leaned back and added: "I believe it's a composite thing of good taste and understanding harmonic structures. It doesn't necessarily mean that they have to "scat" sing at all."

Peg thinks that it's good phrasing and good material that qualifies a capable jazz singer. "That means the voice has to maybe jump a couple of measures—if needed—to re-establish where you started out—always knowing where 'one' is."

Sultry Peggy Lee, formerly Norma Deloris Ekstrom, Big Band singer, instituted the important part of her career when, after slipping into Helen Forrest's shoes with the Benny Goodman band in 1941, she recorded her sulky, jazzy rendition of *Why Don't You Do Right?* in 1942. That recording made her an international star and me a lifelong fan.

Peg really started her professional career quite modestly at the age of fourteen. It was an unheralded debut on local radio station WDAY in Jamestown, North Dakota. It was there that program director Ken Kennedy christened her *Peggy Lee*. She eventually landed a job with the popular novelty band of Will Osborne, the slide-trombonist, vocalist, and drummer leader who composed the swing era hit *Pompton Turnpike*.

In a cocktail lounge at Chicago's Ambassador Hotel shortly before Helen Forrest quit, Benny heard Peggy sing and promptly hired her. After twenty months with Goodman that molded her into one of the most famous female vocalists of the time, Peg and her guitarist husband, former Goodman sideman Dave Barbour, quit the band in 1943 and went on to record a batch of great hits they wrote on their own in the years following, while Peg impersonated a retired, professionally

89

inactive, simple housewife. "Dave would come home," she said, "the dinner wasn't ready—but the songs I worked on all day was."

These are the numbers I most identify with when it comes to Peggy Lee's hits: *It's a Good Day, I Don't Know Enough About You,* and a deft little ditty they composed in 1948 while vacationing in Mexico, *Manana* (it means *tomorrow*), a characterization of sorts where, again, Peggy is acting through the music.

Aside from teaming with her husband, she has written over 500 songs with various collaborators including Broadway's Cy Coleman who penned *Witchcraft* and many other Broadway hits; producer and leader Quincy Jones; orchestra leader and composer Victor Young (*Emily* and *The Shadow of Your Smile composer*), and composer Johnny Mandel. She was careful not to mark them with slang or things that might date the piece so they would not be overtaken by time. "I guess that's an instinct. It's not just good luck to keep a song's standard quality," she noted.

When singing, Peg's voice sort of whispers confidential resonant passion even on the most fragile numbers. Hard songs become dreamy; harsh songs translate into soft songs. Novelty songs become ballads. Some have called her the "Actress of Song." It was Duke Ellington, however, who christened her the "Queen of Song."

In those days, Peggy had always entertained her fellow celebrities and just anyone she knew who wasn't in the business at her lavish home on Kim Ridge Road in Beverly Hills. It was through these parties that Duke Ellington and Peggy got to know one another and became very warm friends. They had always admired one another. Peg had written the lyric for Duke's theme melody for the film *Anatomy Of A Murder*, *Gone Fishin'*. Peg threw a special dinner party for the occasion in the Duke's honor. Charlie Barnet and Frank Sinatra were invited, as was Cary Grant. That party deepened their friendship. At a later gala tribute held at Madison Square Garden and sponsored by the NAACP, so the story goes, Peggy showed up with Quincy Jones to support the Duke. While Peggy was on stage performing, Duke, who was backstage talking with Louis Armstrong, turned to him and said, "Louis, now we really have royalty on that stage. She's the 'Queen.' "

Some critics have suggested Peg emulated the styling of Billie Holiday, but that was impossible. "We had no radio where we lived in

North Dakota," she said, "we didn't even have electricity. When I finally heard Count Basie coming out of Kansas City, I didn't think of it as swing or jazz or anything. It just sounded like good music to me. I can't say I emulated any special singer, until I first heard Maxine Sullivan. She communicated so well—I liked her simplicity." Nat "King" Cole, however, said that when Peg sang *Sometimes I Feel Like a Motherless Child,* she sounded just like Billie Holiday, but Peg just shrugs it off.

Peg always gets very involved in her music, favoring best the theme song she wrote for the 1950 movie *Johnny Guitar*. Her favorite album is *The Man I Love*, recorded in 1957 and orchestrated by musical genius Nelson Riddle, Frank Sinatra's favorite arranger and conductor, and actually conducted by Sinatra himself. One selection, *The Folks Who Live On The Hill*, a quiet, prayerlike piece recorded earlier by Bing Crosby, is a typical reverie style Lee rendition.

When Peggy recorded her swirling, stampeding Decca version of Richard Rodgers' evergreen waltz *Lover*, he was quoted as lamenting, "Oh, my poor little waltz, my little waltz. What happened to my little waltz?" Later, being the very kind and amiable figure he was known to be, he approached Peg: "You can always sing anything of mine." Peg felt that comment from the great composer was quite a compliment.

In a change of pace, Peg's *Is That All There Is?* is a life-weary mystical selection written by rock writers Jerry Leiber & Fred Stoller (who also penned *Hound Dog*) that sticks in your mind and may even keep you awake at night. "Though the song wasn't written for me, it just happened that the lyric paraphrases my life," she said. "I've been through everything including the death experience, but I believe the song is positive. Of course, we all know there *is* more." Few know that Peggy Lee's very early life was that of an abused child at the hand of a cruel step-mother. The abuse that lasted until she was seventeen had an odd effect in that Peggy became a mild, non-violent person, which countermands the expected future life of an abused person. She came to hate violence of every kind.

The story Peg tells of the Capitol recording *You Was Right Baby* was very charming: "It was funny how I got that title. During a record session in Hollywood we heard a crash outside the studio. One of the musicians said, 'I sure hope that wasn't my new car! His girlfriend looked out the window and said, 'You was right, baby!'"

Peg's movie credits include the 1955 *Lady Is a Tramp* where she did four separate voices and sang three individual songs; *Pete Kelly's Blues,* a 1956 film with Jack Webb which earned her an Oscar nomination as a fading nightclub singer, and the 1952 Danny Thomas re-make of *The Jazz Singer.* As a Bing Crosby specialist, I recall a Bing Crosby movie in which Peg appeared. It was a so-so film, the 1950 *Mr. Music,* but, in a peppy party scene, Peg and Bing warble several bubbly choruses of the song *Life Is So Peculiar.* Although her role was just a short cameo, the two entertainers became good friends and singing partners. Peg sang regularly on Bing's radio show for many years afterwards.

"Before I met Bing, I had always secretly loved the Rodgers and Hart song *Down By The River,*" Peg explained, "that he sang years before in (the 1935 film) *Mississippi,* and I told him how I felt about it. One night, when I went to dinner with him to a little place in San Francisco, he actually sang it for me. He somehow convinced the piano player to play it and then sang it for me personally. Can you imagine that? It was a memorable evening. There was always a certain security for me in just thinking about Bing."

It was unfortunate that Peg's own career in films never took off. She certainly can act. It's her one career disappointment. When singing, as I have noted before, she portrays many characterizations. Part singer, part actor, she lives each song according to the character in the lyric. Peggy has, of course, appeared on countless television shows including the one in which a young Frank Sinatra made his debut performance on Bob Hope's second ever TV show.

Peggy Lee is really in a class with counterpart Frank Sinatra. Although she too began her career with the Big Bands, Peg continued her lifelong career as an individual artist choosing her own songs, backup musicians, tailored format, and a very classy wardrobe. Peg has emerged an accomplished and respected, world-class entertainer.

"I learned more about music from the men I worked with in the bands," she says, "than I've learned anywhere else. They taught me discipline and the value of rehearsing and how to train. Even if the interpretation of a particular song wasn't exactly what we wanted, we had to make the best of it."

Peggy has had her share of life's woes on the way to greatness. Four failed marriages (although it is known she always loved best her first husband Dave Barbour, and they were to re-marry when he became suddenly ill and died); two bouts with pneumonia in the Sixties; bypass surgery and even hip surgery in the mid-Eighties (the latter necessitated when performing on-stage with George Burns during a Las Vegas show, when she tripped over a steel plate electrical cover); and surgery on her toes in the late Eighties. This was all balanced by a beautiful daughter, Nicki, now a professional artist (painter of canvasses) in her own right.

"All these ailments are almost like a joke," she says in obvious good spirits. "I think God keeps me around for laughs," she told *Newsday's* Stuart Troup during an interview before a *Ballroom* appearance in New York City.

On March 3, 1994 I received a letter from Ginny Mancini, President of the Society of Singers out in L.A., inviting me to the Beverly Hilton the following May for a celebration honoring Peggy Lee. Many of Peg's friends and colleagues were to be present to honor her with an "Ella" Lifetime Achievement Award. They would acknowledge an astonishing career that included a body of work amounting to over 70 albums as a performer and over 200 copyrighted songs as a lyricist. Only Ella Fitzgerald (in whose honor the award was named), Frank Sinatra, and Tony Martin were previous recipients.

This would be a marvelous, deserving event. And it was! And *everyone* was there. Rosemary Clooney, Jack Jones, Joe Williams, Natalie Cole, and Mel Torme' performed, among others. The Dinner Committee included songwriter Steve Allen, Milton Berle, Steve Lawrence and Eydie Gorme, Gene Kelly, President and Mrs. Ronald Reagan, Jo Stafford & Paul Weston, Johnny Mathis, and Bob Hope. Honorary Chairpersons were Ella Fitzgerald and Frank Sinatra.

Oh, what a tribute to our Peg!

P.S. I almost forgot to mention Peg's stellar version of *Golden Earrings* from the Ray Milland, Marlene Dietrich film of the same name. It's on my personal all-time top ten list.

Rosemary Clooney 1944.
(Richard Grudens Collection)

ROSEMARY CLOONEY

America's Singing Sweetheart

In 1977 Song Star Rosemary Clooney wrote her autobiography in collaboration with author Raymond Strait, entitled *This For Remembrance*. The foreword was composed by her friend and fellow thespian, Bing Crosby, who said, among other things, "Looking back over our long relationship, I have to smile. I'm reminded of all the good times Rosemary and I had together, the fun we had working with the musicians; the kidding, the needling, the ribbing, the laughs-in pictures, radio and television. She's a great singer, and a great lady."

No one could have said it better. Bing and Rosemary Clooney got along just fine and accomplished some terrific recording, radio, television and film sessions together. In Bing's film, *White Christmas*, with co-stars Vera Ellen and Danny Kaye, Rosemary vocalized on two solid selections, *Count Your Blessings*, a definitive Clooney sound, and the best selling song of all time, Irving Berlin's *White Christmas*, dueted with Bing.

As Rosemary described it: "Over the years Bing and I have done the whole entertainment circle together. We were always around each other and became great friends. But, one day I sat down and said to myself, "What the hell am I doing singing here with Bing Crosby?" For her the realization was monumental.

Well, we'll have to turn back a bit to the middle of World War II and the saga of the pretty and lively singing Clooney Sisters, Rosemary and Betty, to discover how that miracle eventually materialized. Long before that book, before life's difficulties, the bad marriages, and the mental shutdown she endured in 1968 that shattered her world; before the five wonderful children, Miguel, Maria, Rafael, Monsita, and Gabriel; and long before she had to fight her way back to a renewed, meaningful life, Rosemary Clooney began her interest-

95

ing journey on a road to becoming a well-loved, world-class Song Star.

As World War II kicked into high gear and defense plants were cooking 24 hours a day, Cincinnati's Keith Albee Theater played host to many of the touring Big Bands. Betty and Rosemary, now living with their maternal grandparents, would be treated to tickets. They all loved to hear the Big Band sounds performed live in their own home town. At the big drug store on Fountain Square, they played the jukebox to the expressive sounds of the Harry James band with Helen Forrest delivering *I've Heard That Song Before* and Kitty Kallen emotionalizing for the hopeful return of their loved ones singing "Kiss me once and kiss me twice, and kiss me once again, It's Been A Long, Long, Time."

With a three-song repertoire, the girls auditioned for a job with WLW, a Cincinnati radio station, and copped a twenty-dollar-a-week (for each girl) job. They moved in with their Aunt Jean in the city close to the studio, slept on the couch while simultaneously attending Our Lady Of Mercy Academy, saving more money Rosemary said, "than when I was making $20,000 a week in later years." In a local band fronted by a trumpet-playing friend, the girls became *bona fide* Big Band singers. They were billed as the Clooney Sisters. They soon joined up with Doris Day's old big band affiliation, the popular Barney Rapp Band, who played bigger club dates in the area. Next stop, a stint with former Artie Shaw sideman, bandleader Tony Pastor, who had just started up.

The butterflies were starting; they were in the big-time now. Rosemary was eighteen and Betty just fifteen. They looked great in their twin dresses. It's simply amazing how early in life most of the Song Stars began their professional careers. Billie Holiday, Ella Fitzgerald, Connie Haines, Kitty Kallen, Doris Day, Helen O'Connell, Fran Warren, and some others were teen-agers all. They literally grew up on the bandstand and spent a good portion of their lives sleeping in the band buses, motels and hotels.

The Steel Pier in Atlantic City was their first Pastor engagement, and it was also their first look at an ocean. "We were so excited, we never slept." Rosemary said, "We studied our lead sheets and rehearsed and rehearsed. It was make-it-or-break-it time for us." The chaperone was their Uncle George, steadfastly assigned to them by their grandmother. One-night stands that followed were held at college proms, barn dances, subscription dances, hotel ballrooms, dance pavilions, and theaters.

"After each show, we would climb aboard our chartered bus and sleep until we arrived at the next place where we did another show," Rosemary remembered. During that time, the girls took their first plane trip. They were headed for the Hollywood Palladium.

When Rosemary got off the plane, she fell instantly in love with California's soft air and warm climate and would come to love California for the remainder of her life.

During that period, after recording an album with Tony Pastor, Rosemary received a great review from *Downbeat Magazine*, which said: "Rosemary Clooney has an extraordinarily good voice, perhaps the nearest thing to Ella Fitzgerald's we've ever heard." Rosie literally flipped out. "After that review everything changed." And according to Tony Pastor in George Simon's book *The Big Band Era:* "They were smart kids," he said, "They had good ears and some corny arrangements of their own. But Ralph Flanagan (later to lead a Glenn Miller style band), who was writing for us, gave them some good new arrangements, and they did just fine."

I remember one particular movie short (pre-MTV) with Tony and Rosemary dueting on a cute little song entitled *Movie Tonight*. A great Clooney performance where shades of Helen Forrest and Anita O'Day can be distinguished from within this very new Song Star to be. Tony moved her right along, and Rosemary carried her share off very well. The camera loved her bright face and eager smile.

"After three or so years of band bus traveling," Rosemary noted, "Betty decided to quit and I remained with Tony as a single. Even Uncle George went home with her."

That's when Rosemary developed her easy and friendly singing manner. Her first solo recording in 1946 was "*I'm Sorry I Didn't Say I'm Sorry When I Made You Cry Last Night*"—whew, what a long title. It was noticed by radio disc jockeys everywhere as something special, but Rosemary explained: "I was so scared that I couldn't sing above a whisper. They seemed to like that sound which I created through my own fear," she said, smiling inwardly. Rosemary never sounded quite like that again.

Teaming up with personal manager Joe Shribman, who managed Tony Pastor, Rosemary launched a career on her own. Tony Bennett enlightened me about it somewhat when he and I talked about some of the singers of his time: "Her big break came on a show you may remember called Jan Murray's *Songs For Sale* in 1950. Rosemary won hands down—I came in second—on Arthur Godfrey's Talent Scouts which won her a "gig" on Jan Murray's show, *Songs For Sale*. She was simply great!" This led to more engagements and the popularization of an earlier Columbia recording, a resplendent version of *Beautiful Brown Eyes*. In 1951, song pioneer Mitch Miller, the visionary A & R man at Columbia Records and the man responsible for the success of many singers including Tony Bennett, Frankie Laine, and Guy Mitchell, convinced Rosemary to record a bouncy number with the unusual name of *Come On-a My House*, an adaptation by William Saroyan and Ross Bagdasarian of an old Armenian folk song.

"I didn't want to do such a unromantic, silly number," Rosemary said, "I was a ballad singer, and I hated that song. I thought it was a cheap way to get attention. But he insisted and threatened to fire me if I didn't show up at the studio. Well, it turned out he was right." In a few weeks the song became a national best-selling record. "Who else could have put a harpsichord on a Clooney record (*Come On-a My House*) or backed Guy Mitchell with swooping French horns (*My Truly, Truly Fair*)?" Frankie Laine said when we talked about Miller's influence on singing careers.

"That's true," cited Rosemary, "Mitch could bring people together. He was a hit-maker. A lot of us started together: Tony Bennett, Frankie Laine, Guy Mitchell at Columbia; Patti Page at Mercury; Doris Day and Dinah Shore also at Columbia. Mitch was there making sure everything sounded right."

Rosemary's first important job was a date at the Chicago Theater with Frankie Laine. "Frankie had left Mercury and was now recording with Columbia, and we did seven shows a day because Frankie was very, very hot."

Her subsequent recordings kept topping the music charts: the moving song she loved so much, *Hey There* (which is my and, also, was WNEW disc jockey William B. Williams' favorite Clooney recording from Richard Adler and Jerry Ross' Broadway show *Pajama Game)*; the lighthearted *Botcha Me; This Old House;* and the perky *Mambo Italiano*. With husband Jose Ferrer, she recorded the selections *A Bunch Of Bananas* and *Woman* and with world-famous actress and friend, Marlene Dietrich, *Dot's Nice—Don na Fight*, a cute little ditty. Hank Williams' *Half As Much* is also a commendable Clooney specialty as is one of her best and most successful recordings, *Tenderly,* which appears over and over again on Top Ten lists of great recordings of the era including the 1996 WQEW top tunes of the last 60 years.

While working on the Tallulah Bankhead Sunday radio show, I remember Rosemary at a rehearsal in the Center Theater, across the street from the NBC studios on West 49th Street (the theater is now gone). The *Big Show* was the last great resistance of radio to the new monster called television. It was underwritten by then mega-sponsors Reynolds Metals, Anacin, and Chesterfield Cigarettes with Tallulah as Mistress of Ceremonies. The greatest talent of the times appeared on that show. It was where President Harry Truman's daughter, Margaret, appeared for the first time as a professional vocalist. It was on that day, April 13, 1952, that Rosemary met her future friend, *Blue Angel* and *Golden Earrings* motion picture icon Marlene Dietrich. She enthusiastically complimented Rosemary's singing while offering encouragement and suggesting they remain in touch with one another. They did and became good friends.

Under contract to Paramount, given full opportunity to display both her verve and voice, a successful, young and peppy Rosemary Clooney began a movie career. First, *The Stars are Singing*, then *Here Comes The Girls* with my friend Bob Hope, singer Tony Martin, and Arlene Dahl. This refreshing and attractive Song Star followed up with *Red Garters*, *Deep In My Heart*, and in 1954, *White Christmas*— for my money the most memorable Rosemary Clooney movie. She was at her best in voice and looks and even learned to execute some remarkable dancing routines.

Released from Paramount and now free as a bird, television beckoned the former big band singer and movie star. It was regular appearances on *The Steve Allen Show*, Perry Como's show, Ed Sullivan's *Toast Of The Town,* and a special with master-arranger and special friend, Nelson Riddle and his Orchestra.

Her own show, *The Rosemary Clooney Show,* debuted in May, 1956, over KKTV in L.A., quickly networking to New York in only a few months. A gracious hostess with that appealing husky throat, Rosemary's musical pleasantries handily carried the TV torch.

"I tried to strive for intimacy by playing not to a studio audience but to just one or two people looking in," she explained to me one night in Huntington, New York's Heckscher Park back in 1984 just before an outdoor performance. Unfortunately that night our interview was cut short by her road manager, Alan Sviridoff, because he felt Rosemary was somewhat over-tired from excessive trecking around on one—night stands and had to go on stage shortly. It was a very hot August evening, indeed, and Rosemary was indeed gracious and apologetic. Alan extended me a backstage invitation for later that October during an upcoming appearance with Tony Bennett at the Westbury Music Fair just a few miles away.

In 1956, Rosemary scored with Duke Ellington as a jazz singer, no less. Characterized with jazz surroundings and the effects of Johnny Hodges'sax, Cat Anderson's trumpet, and the trumpets of Clark Terry and Ray Nance she sang *Grievin',* a beautiful jazz recording written and arranged by Billy Strayhorn. In my opinion, it's one of Rosemary's best recordings ever. Try to find a copy of it. You'll love it. It's a different Rosie.

Some twenty-five years later, it would be more jazz for Rosemary Clooney with young jazz stars Warren Vache and Scott Hamilton. Today, all her work is arranged by John Oddo, who also supervised young Tom Postilio's first album, *What Matters Most,* and his subsequent appearances at New York's Tavern On The Green during the summer of 1996.

Rosemary has, of course, recorded endless singles, many children's records along the way, and albums—lots of albums. Some with Bing Crosby, Les Brown, her good friend Buddy Cole and his Trio, Tony Bennett, Woody Herman, Scott Hamilton, and Nelson Riddle, mostly on RCA. On the Concord label, it's been recordings of mostly small group jazz albums in tributes to the great song writers. During the late '70's and early '80's it was the "4 girls 4" tour with Song Stars Margaret Whiting, Helen O'Connell, and Kay Starr.

And, yes, she still is swinging today. Just a week ago, in September, 1996, Rosemary appeared on Carnegie Hall's hallowed stage in a fitting commemorative tribute to the master arranger, Nelson Riddle, with John Oddo directing the music under the auspices of the Concord Jazz Festival.

There's a lot that can be said about Rosemary Clooney's private life, but it will be best left to her own definitive autobiography, *This For Remembrance*. "Today," she says, "my life is pretty darn good—although not without problems like anyone's life, but I can deal with them." Some say that parts of Rosemary Clooney's life were a special hell, "but without that," she added, "I would not know joy—and that is what I feel today."

Rosemary Clooney's life today is an endless happy ending. She shares grandchildren with Pat Boone, Song Star in his own right, who has been Rosemary's neighbor for many years. Neighborhood kid Gabriel Ferrer married childhood sweetheart Debbie Boone. Pat, his wife Shirley, and Rosemary (the consummate home entertainer to friends and relatives) enjoy the bounty that is called *family*.

At this writing (late December, 1996) Rosemary Clooney is touring, landing next week at the Sands Hotel and Casino in Atlantic City, New Jersey, in a show she calls *Rosemary Clooney's White Christmas*. She sounds better and better, but she *will* be home for Christmas.

**Teresa Brewer and New York Yankees great Micky Mantle 1953.
(Bob Thiele Collection)**

TERESA BREWER

So Much Music, Music, Music

Bette Midler speaks out about one of her heroes, Song Star Teresa Brewer: "Most contemporary singers give credit to the Beatles, the Stones and Elvis. My inspiration came from Patti Page, Jo Stafford and Teresa Brewer. Actually, the record *Till I Waltz Again With You* was instrumental in setting me in my path."

A very favorable commentary indeed to launch a chapter about a child prodigy from Toledo, Ohio, who began her career singing *Take Me Out To The Ball Game* over radio station WSPD on *Uncle August's Kiddie Show*. She was just over two. Her pay was cupcakes and cookies. Nobody believed her age. At the time, the name was Theresa Breuer, but it's been Teresa Brewer for a long time now.

At age five Teresa won a spot on the *Major Bowes Amateur Hour* traveling radio program. She toured with the show, singing and dancing like crazy for seven years. It all came naturally to her: "We traveled by bus sometimes," said Teresa, "but usually by train. They rented the entire car and we'd take the seats apart and would make beds. I made one hundred dollars a week, more than anyone else in the unit. I sent home $25.00 and kept $75.00 for expenses." They would go out for two weeks and come back home for four weeks, then go out over and over again.

At twelve, Teresa's parents curtailed the touring and sent her back to Toledo's Holy Rosary School, but she kept active as a performer. "I quit two months before graduation because I could not stand it any longer. All I wanted to do was perform. I didn't need a diploma. What would I do with it in the music business?" Teresa performed on local radio shows and eventually starred in her own show as *Toledo's Miss Talent*.

Beginning sixteen years after that first auspicious performance, Teresa held the entire country in her palms with two terrific recordings, *Music, Music, Music* in 1949 and *Till I Waltz Again With You* in 1952. She was but nineteen. Bing Crosby called her the "Sophie Tucker of the

Teresa Brewer sent us this cute photo of her early performances.

Girl Scouts," observing that giant voice in proportion to that small body, and Pat Boone told me once that Teresa absolutely encouraged him to pursue a singing career.

Arranging for Teresa Brewer's appearance in *Song Stars*, I consulted with Bill Munroe, Teresa's Fan Club President from New Haven, Connecticut. Bill was first an early avid Teresa Brewer collector and eventually became a personal friend. His association with Teresa and her husband, Bob Thiele, reaches back to the early 1970's. Bill was able to supply an assortment of photos and a complete update on her latest activities.

Although Teresa did not originate as a Big Band Singer, she has simply reversed the process. She did sing with Ted Lewis' band, and then, in the latter part of her career, joined with Duke Ellington's *It Don't Mean A Thing If It Ain't Got That Swing* album of Ellington songs produced in 1974. It was the last studio album he recorded. Then, under the direction of his son Mercer, she recorded the hits of the Cotton Club era. It continued with the albums *The Songs of Bessie Smith* recorded with the one and only Count Basie, then kept going strong with Benny Carter and also Earl Hines on a Fats Waller Tribute. The album, *Teresa Brewer and Friends, Memories of Louis,* was performed with stellar trumpeters Harry "Sweets" Edison, Dizzy Gillespie, Clark Terry, Ruby Braff, Wynton Marsalis, and Freddie Hubbard. Bob Thiele produced. What an extraordinary lineup! What an astonishing cluster of players! On the album *What A Wonderful World* Teresa manipulated her voice in an exquisite vocal outlay with pianist Hank Jones, bassist George Duvivier, and jazz violinist Stephane Grappelli. Those are regal Big Band credentials.

The days have been harrowing lately for Teresa with the loss last January of her devoted husband of twenty-three years, Bob Thiele. They were very close to one another.

Bob's own career covered a wide range of music endeavors. He had produced some notable works with the legendary jazz sax player John Coltrane and other jazz stars. An amateur clarinetist who struck an early interest in jazz, he became a jazz oriented radio disc jockey. Bob edited and published *Jazz Magazine* from 1939 to 1941, and owned and operated Signature Records from 1940 through 1948. He also co-composed the charming and infectious tune *What a Wonderful World*,

Teresa Brewer with Duke Ellington 1974. (Courtesy Columbia Records)

recorded by Louis Armstrong and revised recently as the background theme in the film *Good Morning, Vietnam* that starred Robin Williams.

Bob was also Teresa's biggest fan, producing many of her recordings, "and he helped make our world a bit more wonderful to live in, too." Teresa added warmly, "He had a good heart. Please remember him in your prayers."

At her home in New Rochelle, New York, Teresa elucidated about the flip side of a recording entitled *Copenhagen,* initiated in late 1949 on London Records, a fledgling English label trying to break into the American market. Its name *Music! Music! Music!*, sometimes titled *Put Another Nickel In.* How many times have *you* heard that recording? Perhaps a hundred, maybe a thousand or more times. It's one of those second-nature tunes you can never forget, even if you haven't heard it for a while. It becomes implanted in your brain forever.

"It was a German-type song," she told me, "and when it was played to me the first time, I told them I could not sing that song. The tempo is just too slow. But, I did it...and, of course, I'm glad I did. London Records was just starting to sign American artists, but the records were actually pressed in England. There was a strike over there when *Music, Music* came out and we couldn't get the records pressed. It sold over a million, but it could have sold much, much more if there hadn't been a strike. Still, it kicked off my recording career rather nicely!"

> *Put another nickel in,*
> *In the nickelodeon*
> *All I want is loving you*
> *And music, music, music.*

It's ironic and amusing that, although Teresa actually prefers Dixieland jazz, blues and ballads, she wound up singing those bouncy, upbeat tunes and acquired a reputation for them, and thus achieving everlasting fame.

"That was my 'ootsy-poo' period. That's *all* they gave me," she went on, "Some of those records should have been children's records." The 1950's *Molasses, Molasses* and *Choo'n Gum* "were icky, sticky," Teresa declared in her homespun jargon, "and they were hits. *Molasses* was my favorite song to sing my children to sleep. I would bounce them on the bed or tuck them in to sleep, so that was great. They were the first songs my girls ever knew." Her four now grown daughters are Kathleen, Susan, Megan, and Michelle.

Next, we spoke about that other evergreen, *Till I Waltz Again With You*: "The first time I heard it, I thought it was a very pretty song. I met its writer in an elevator in New York. He sang the song for me as we were going up in the elevator. He sang it in country tempo-you know, with an extra fifth bar. I said it just doesn't work. It was called *Till I Waltz Again With You* and it wasn't even a waltz! But it was beautiful so we put in a 'pop' meter...and it was a hit, too," then, beaming, "I think it's my favorite of all that I had." That ballad became 1953's best-selling recording.

During that year, Paramount Pictures ran a poll to locate the country's most popular girl singer for an upcoming movie, *Those Redheads From Seattle*. Teresa, with her exceptional looks and immense popularity, won, got screen-tested, and appeared in the film. But, because family life remained first in her mind, she rejected a subsequent lucrative seven-year film contract, keeping her nestled in her New Rochelle East Coast home, which is filled with personal, beloved antique furniture and glassware collected on trips around the world. Being close to New York City she could conveniently appear on live network television and generate many more recordings.

The year 1953 saw the release of another Brewer all-time favorite, *Ricochet*: "*Ricochet* was not supposed to be released—at least not that particular take," she explained, "In those days, it wasn't on tape and everything had to be right at the same time—the orchestra, vocalist, everything. I had a bad cold," she continued, "and didn't like the way it turned out. We redid it another day, but Bob Thiele (Teresa's husband to be and Coral Records' A & R man at the time) released the first take—the one with *my* cold." It's funny, but it seemed as though everything Teresa rejected at the time became a hit for her.

"*Let Me Go Lover*," Teresa recalled, "was the theme song from a TV show. The program was on at nine o'clock and we were in the studio recording that song at two o'clock that very morning. It was an instant hit for me...and Patti Page too." And about the song *A Tear Fell*: "Now I *loved* that song. It was originally a rhythm and blues record. At that time, the R & B artist just couldn't break out in the pop music world. So everybody, every pop artist, was covering R & B records. I felt a little guilty about it because they had better records out than we made. But the songs were so great that the pop artists did them too."

As a long-time New York Yankees baseball fan, I enjoy the affectionate ditty *I Love Mickey*, which was co-authored and recorded by Teresa. "I understand that Mickey Mantle was also a Teresa Brewer fan," I reminded Teresa. "Yes, he was!" says she. This recording is now one of the most collectible of all her recordings.

Television guest-star Brewer ran the gamut of the tubes on a profusion of the best known variety shows: Ed Sullivan's *Toast Of The Town* (over 30 times—a record, I think), Perry Como's premier show, and *Arthur Godfrey and His Friends,* too. In the following 20 years or so there have been 20 albums, some bursting at the seams with jazz. The last person to come to mind when you think of great jazz singers would be Teresa Brewer, but, she clarified, "My husband, Bob, taught me to appreciate jazz. He didn't try to change me, but he would ask, 'Could you do such and such a thing?' "

Her collaboration with Dizzy Gillespie on the selection *St.Louis Blues* in the 1991 album *Teresa Brewer & Friends, Memories of Louis*, is a classic. In the New York Daily News, jazz writer Hugh Wyatt wrote: "This recording is one for the *Guinness Book*. She has made a successful transition to jazz." Her unique voice was apparently well suited to the jazz idiom of American music.

So, in what category is Teresa Brewer? Pop Singer, Big Band Singer, Jazz Singer? Bandleader Larry Elgart told me she defies classification. "You can't pigeonhole Teresa Brewer." Always surprising, can sing anything, any way you want it. A Carnegie Hall performance in 1978, a command performance for British Royalty in 1985, she's done it all on over 75 albums and countless singles.

Teresa has four daughters and two grandchildren. "They're gorgeous," she said.

Teresa Brewer may first have earned fame as a child prodigy, but she's a real Song Star now. She is simply wonderful. We can't wait until Teresa gets her career going again. Wasn't it Scarlet O'Hara who said, "Tomorrow is another day"? You'll be hearing again from Teresa very soon. You can bet your last nickel on it.

Lena Horne and Noble Sissle, Circa 1935.
(Photo D. Schiedt)

LENA HORNE

Song Star with a Message

In October, 1944, Lena Horne, premier singer and actress, became the first black person to appear on the cover of a popular movie magazine. What a long way she had come. Her great ambition had been to use a God-given talent and hard-won success to win respect for her race. Lena Horne always envisioned a better heritage for her people. That meant financial, economic, and cultural advantages. Her lifetime hero and mentor was opera singer and entertainer Paul Robeson. Inspiring refusals to play black stereotype roles in movies broke new ground.

My friend William B. Williams worshipped Lena Horne. He would always talk about her and regularly played her recordings on his show *The Make Believe Ballroom*, a popular radio show on New York's WNEW during the '60's, '70's, and '80's. He drawled huskily, "Lena,"—and everyone knew exactly whom he meant. When she appeared in a one-woman Broadway show during the early 1980's, he consistently promoted it on the show. She was also a regular in-person guest.

Lena Horne surfaces from a great family that dates back to 1777 in the state of Maryland. Over one hundred years later Cora and Edwin Horn (the *e* added later) moved to New York City in 1896. They settled in the area between Sixteenth and Sixty-fifth Streets, West of Seventh Avenue, in an area known as San Juan Hill near the Grand Opera House on Eighth Avenue. During the Twenties you might have seen early jazz artist Jelly Roll Morton, or even Scott Joplin himself, headline there.

This was the young couple's first Northern home after their 1887 marriage in Chattanooga, Tennessee, although Cora originally came from Birmingham, Alabama. Edwin was a teacher and editor of a local paper in Chattanooga, as well as a partner in a local drug store, but gave it all up because of the recent terrorist practices against blacks in the region. When their area of New York City became a rough and dangerous neighborhood, the couple moved across the river into nearby Brooklyn, taking up residence on Chauncey Street, near the exciting and modern Bushwick Avenue.

Edwin taught in the New York City public school system, became a factor in the early fight for equality, and was an early member, with his wife, of the NAACP.

Their two small sons, Errol and Teddy, grew up very differently from one another, so we shall concentrate on Teddy, who was a rip-roaring young man of the Roaring Twenties and future father of Lena. Teddy married Edna, a black "princess"—a fantasist, a freckled, green-eyed minx. She had known Teddy all his life. Our Song Star Lena Mary Calhoun Horne was born to the union on June 30, 1917, in a small Jewish lying-in hospital. It was the year Scott Joplin died and the year *The New York Times* first used the word *jazz*. (Lt. Errol Horne went to France in 1918 and perished from influenza instead of bullets.)

Lena began her illustrious career in 1919, becoming a cover girl at the age of two-and-a-half, starring in the October, 1919, issue of the *NAACP Branch Bulletin*. Her father Teddy left his Brooklyn home and went west in the summer of 1920, leaving his family and Chauncey Street where they had lived with his parents. He claimed the need for dry air was necessary to cure his acknowledged breathing difficulties. Marriage and family stability was not his life's interest.

After a somewhat difficult life of being shunted from city to city, her mother constantly running from her father, Lena sometimes stayed with her mother and sometimes with her grandmother. It was Miami, then Jacksonville, and back to Brooklyn again. Next, it was Ohio, to be left with a middle-class doctor's family, sharing a top floor room with a maiden aunt, and then on to Macon, Georgia, to be left with two old women. She finally migrated to Fort Valley, near Macon, with her Uncle Frank Horne. Lena grew to love Fort Valley, but was truly a Horne of Chauncey Street, Brooklyn, where she was sure of who she was.

It was in the Junior Guild of Brooklyn's annual charity show where Lena landed her first starring role. She had the biggest part and sang all the best songs: *Night and Day* and *I've Got the World on a String*. As a result her photograph appeared in all the local papers. It was nothing but *bravo* reviews. Then Edna, her mother, had a secret plan. She knew the dance captain at the world-famous Cotton Club in Harlem, and, although Lena was only seventeen, she was able to get her a spot in the show's New Revue. The Cotton Club was a great Harlem nightspot built by gangsters in a time when speak-easys prevailed in the big cities. It was *the* place to go. Duke Ellington, Cab Calloway, and the great Louis Armstrong were featured performers. Anyone who was anyone went to the Cotton Club: actors George Raft and Greta Garbo, violin genius Jascha Heifetz, Britain's Lord Mountbatten, baseball's Babe Ruth, and entertainer Eddie Cantor, who once said that if he were elected President he'd hold the Inaugural Ball at the Cotton Club.

The Cotton Club was *jazz*. It was gangsters and booze and beautiful black women. It was where Ethel Waters first sang the great Harold Arlen song *Stormy Weather* that the young Lena Horne would later come to be associated with in the movies. On her so-so debut, Lena's photo appeared in the *Amsterdam News*.

Now the pet of the Cotton Club, "protected" by the Dutch Schultz mob who owned Harlem, Lena earned twenty-five dollars a week. She became everybody's kid sister and once sang in place of Aida Ward, a Cotton Club star who had a sore throat. Lena sang *As Long As I Live* in place of the ailing Aida. Lena was beginning to be noticed. Her father even came to see her, although he was black and not allowed to sit among the strictly white audience. He was so well—regarded by the Cotton Club owners that they permitted him to watch from a special section. Lena was awestruck by the Cotton Club, the wealth of the patrons, and the notoriety of its owners. The nightclub was a large horseshoe-shaped room with tables on two levels and booths against all the walls. Mexican and Chinese food was always served, except for fried chicken after hours.

Her second break came in the fall of 1934 when Broadway producer Laurence Schwab, who noticed her in the Cotton Club chorus line, cast her as a quadroon as part of a voodoo ballet in a show called *Dance with Your Gods*.

After *Gods* closed, Lena viewed the club in a more realistic light. "I saw that twenty-five of us were herded into one tiny, crowded, windowless dressing room in which we had barely enough space to sit down. It stunk from ashtrays, newspapers, make-up, fan magazines, cartons of stale chop suey and the reek of perfume and cigarette smoke. I longed for a breath of fresh air and some place I could stretch my aching limbs and go to sleep." But Lena was otherwise grateful for the job.

After that show, her mother Edna badgered the Cotton Club management for a better show spot for her daughter, but was refused. Lena was defensively whisked out of the Club by friends, against the wishes of the controlling mob. She joined Noble Sissle's sweet band, a favorite of the black middle-class and older whites. They went on the road, her mother traveling right along. Sissle helped improve Lena's act. He taught her to properly phrase a song and perfected her diction, confirming his well-known dedication to imparting poise and polish in a vocalist. Sissle was very happy with Lena whom he renamed Helene Horne. Together, they were a class act.

In 1936 Sissle's orchestra was the first black band to play at the famous Ritz-Carlton in Boston. Lena sang the winsome *Blue Moon* and developed a following, mostly students from nearby Harvard University.

John Hammond, a rich young man devoted to the promotion of jazz and its performers, noticed Lena. He, of course, was the angel responsible for the promotion of Benny Goodman, Count Basie, and Billie Holiday, to name a few, and the catalyst behind the 1938 Benny Goodman Concert that brought respectability to jazz music.

At this time the very pretty Lena was introduced to twenty-eight year old Louis Jones of Pittsburgh. Lena was charmed by his good manners and favorable position in life and decided to marry him. She settled down and became pregnant with her daughter Gail.

Lena went to Hollywood to make a film she never got paid for, returned to New York, and was cast in the short-lived *Blackbirds of 1939* on Broadway to great revues. Then Lena received a break. Bandleader Charlie Barnet was appearing in the Bronx and his girl singer took sick:

"Wow! Who are *you*?" were Charlie's first encouraging words to Lena Horne when she applied for the job. As Big Band crooner Bob Carroll tells it: "We were working at the Windsor Theater in the Bronx (N.Y.) and something had happened to the girl we were using. Somebody remembered this pretty girl who was working in a movie house, and they sent for her. It was Lena. I remember she had long, straggly hair, and her dress wasn't especially attractive. She ran down a few tunes in the basement of the theater, and then, without any arrangements, she did the next show—not only did it, but stopped it cold. She was just great." Lena was accepted, touring on the road once again as the girl singer in a big band.

Traumatic racial incidents befell the young star: Most hotels had a "No Blacks Allowed" policy and sometimes Charlie threatened to pull the whole band out. At times it worked. At college dances, Charlie would be told that Lena was unacceptable, so she got the night off. Other times she could sing, but not sit on the bandstand. On Southern tours, Lena was given vacation with pay.

Once, while waiting, she recorded with bandleader Artie Shaw who had heard her sing *Good for Nothing Joe*. The record *Don't Take Your Love from Me* was waxed. In frustration Lena quit Barnet and moved back to her beloved Chauncey Street home. The marriage to Louis was virtually over even though her second child, Teddy, was born after a short reconciliation that never lasted. Louis was too domineering for the independent spirit that was Lena Horne.

John Hammond was instrumental in getting Lena a job in Cafe' Society, one of New York's most notable clubs, where he was chief talent scout. It was an unsegregated nightclub that helped launch the careers of Josh White, Zero Mostel, Billie Holiday, Hazel Scott, and Judy Holiday.

Lena first met Billie Holiday backstage at Kelly's Stable, which was also located in Greenwich Village. They immediately took a liking to one another. They conferred and compared. Lena opened at Cafe' Society with the fine Teddy Wilson band and sang Billie's *Fine and Mello* and George Gershwin's beautiful *Summertime*. Her *Summertime* song was performed so well that every critic noticed and bestowed praises in their columns and on the radio.

That launched Lena's career. Then a Carnegie Hall show with Teddy Wilson, Count Basie, Bunny Berigan, and Hazel Scott, among others, boosted her even higher. Here Lena first met her mentor, singer Paul Robeson, and her new boyfriend, boxer Joe Louis. Teddy Horne, an insider in the Champ's circle of friends, played a role in

1942 MGM film promotion poster *Cabin in the Sky*.
(Richard Grudens Collection)

116

that meeting. It was a mercurial, celebrity romance that ended just as quickly. Lena was now 23.

It was on to California to work the opening of a new club, the Trocadero, fashioned after the Cotton Club. Lena was invited to attend a performance by her new friend Duke Ellington, who was appearing in a show called *Jump for Joy* in Los Angeles. There she met Ellington sidekick, composer and pianist Billy Strayhorn and became his lifelong friend, sister and soul mate. Billy re-arranged Lena's entire repertoire, shaping her into a major attraction at local night clubs. Duke Ellington thought Lena a delicate beauty. The Hollywood crowd loved her, too. There were admirers Cole Porter, Marlene Dietrich, John Barrymore, and Roger Edens, chief of musicals at MGM, who attended those shows. Lena soon found herself a member of the MGM "stable of stars."

Under the influence of the NAACP Lena became the force for blacks in Hollywood. Their time had come. The gong had rung itself out on stereotype black players. Meanwhile, Lena went to work at the Mocambo on the Sunset Strip and was a smash. Humble and elegant, Lena prevailed as an artist of stature. Soon it was the definitive songs *Honeysuckle Rose* and *Brazilian Boogie* in movies directed by Vincente Minnelli that endeared her to the public.

A happy Lena moved into a new house surrounded by eucalyptus trees and geraniums, although she always maintained her disdain for California. Starring in the 1942 movie *Cabin in the Sky* with Ethel Waters and Eddie "Rochester" Anderson, also directed by Minnelli, Lena was the darling of the technical crew, but was equally despised by a jealous Ethel Waters who caused continuous trouble for her on the set. Despite that, the film, that also starred Duke Ellington, Eddie "Rochester" Anderson, and Bill "Bojangles" Robinson, established a new kind of image for black women in the movies. It opened in New York at the Capitol Theater. Duke Ellington and Lena appeared on stage as live show attractions. The show and movie were a smash. There were lines around the block.

Lonely for New York, Lena returned with an engagement at the Savoy Plaza Persian Room, being the first black entertainer to play the room. Ironically, she had her own room to rest and change in but could not stay overnight. She took that in stride and was an absolute

**Lena sings Harold Arlen's *Stormy Weather* from 1943 Fox film.
(Richard Grudens Collection)**

success. Someone said she would need Madison Square Garden for her next stand. *Time*, *Newsweek* and *Life* held features on Lena all in the same week in January, 1943.

Lena unselfishly worked the USO and Hollywood Canteens to entertain and serve coffee and doughnuts to lonely servicemen. "It made me happy to contribute something to our fighting men," she said.

In 1943, the landmark Lena Horne film, *Stormy Weather*, directed by Andrew Stone (instead of MGM's Vincent Minnelli), was produced by Twentieth Century Fox. There was a story that because Lena did not like Bill Robinson—considering him a male version of Ethel Waters—she was unable to get into character and cry during a certain scene with Robinson. I still think she sang that song best in the film. Future versions were never as genuine.

Back in Hollywood, Lena first met her husband-to-be, studio conductor Lennie Hayton, at lunch in the studio commissary. "At first we didn't get along," she said, "but we quickly became a twosome. Lennie would write special arrangements—he suited me musically—he stretched me musically We dug each other...were always in tune with one another." Lennie directed music at MGM. He was formerly pianist-arranger for Paul Whiteman's King of Jazz Orchestra. He arranged music for legendary jazz cornetist Bix Beiderbecke, trumpeter Bunny Berigan, trombonist Jack Teagarden, the Dorsey Brothers, and Bing Crosby, who were all members of the orchestra. Lennie and Lena worked together on the 1946 Jerome Kern musical film *Till the Clouds Roll By* in which Lena sang *Why Was I Born* and fellow performer Frank Sinatra sang *Ol' Man River*.

Lennie and Lena decided to get married. It would isolate her from the world. It was illegal for whites and blacks to marry in California in 1946, "...and," she said, "Hollywood society began to cold-shoulder us." So the couple went east. It was hotels and more hotels in New York City. They traveled to Europe, the war being over, and viewed war-torn London. Lena appeared with Ted Heath's big band at the London Casino. As one of the first American performers to play postwar London, Lena was a great success. England was very familiar with her Big Band performances and movies. In Paris, it was appearances at the Club des Champs-Elysees, near the Arc de Triomphe.

Lena befriended Song Star Edith Piaf and actors Simone Signoret and Piaf protege' Yves Montand. Lennie and Lena secretly married in Paris and then sailed home.

Lennie continued his work as MGM musical director on a batch of new movies: *Good News, The Barkleys of Broadway*, and *Words and Music* (in which Lena appeared), while Lena was invited to sing at Harry S. Truman's Presidential Inauguration. In 1950 they revealed their marriage to the press, and thus the world, and sailed once again to Europe. Lena performed at the Palladium as the Korean War broke out. She toured the English Isles. For the rest of the decade, the couple would be regular European summer residents.

Lena Horne led a quasi-political life. Leave it to say that Lena worked hard to advance the cause of civil rights to obtain justice for her race in meaningful and positive ways for all her life and was very much admired for it. In 1960 on the cover of *Show* magazine, the cover read: "Breaking the white barrier: Lena Horne speaks on the artist and the negro revolt." She was a great example and an outspoken champion. It was dedicated, never-ending work.

Lena's appearances on television with her friends Ed Sullivan, Perry Como, Steve Allen, and Tex and Jinx McCrary (also my old friends from early NBC days in New York) were many, although a show of her own was out of the question in those days. Although Lena made lots of money in nightclubs, she really didn't like performing in them. She appeared at the Sands in Las Vegas in the mid-'50's among all the other great names. Only Lena, Sinatra and Danny Thomas, however, had their names framed on the Sands brochures. They were the "royalty" acts of the clubs.

Lena appeared on Broadway once again, this time in a 1957 musical *Jamaica,* as its star. The consensus was: "Lena plus music equals a BIG winner." Lena remained the queen of the nightclubs long after *Jamaica* folded.

Lena's 1981 hit Broadway show *Lena Horne: The Lady and Her Music,* the show William B. Williams helped promote on his WNEW radio show, was the best of the season. It ran 14 months to sellout crowds. Reviews were absolutely superlative. She had been rediscovered. "I was a different Lena...at last a free Lena," she said to me.

Lena has won just about every award possible including the coveted Kennedy Center Honors along with comedian Danny Kaye, composer Gian Carlo Mennotti, (I worked on his very first *Amahl and The Night Visitors* groundbreaking television operetta in 1952 at NBC studio 9B), playwright Arthur Miller, and classical violinist Isaac Stern.

This vignette about Lena Horne's life is partly drawn from, among other sources, her daughter Gail Lumet Buckley's book *The Hornes-An American Family*. It is a treatise on a wonderful family and was a pleasure to read and re-read. It was a great help in organizing Lena's life for *Song Stars*.

Lena is growing older most gracefully surrounded by her family who all live close to her Manhattan apartment. "My family is closest to my heart," she said. Lena reads a lot—my stuff too, I hope, enjoys her grandchildren and great-grandchildren, and at 79 takes in an occasional concert or play.

PBS has currently featured her in their Biography series, *Lena Horne*: *In Her Own Voice*. It was produced by Susan Lacy and traces Lena's life and career on film. At a screening of that show at the Hilton Room (formerly the Empire Room where she played in the 50's) Lena summed it all up with this self-effacing statement: "I guess it wasn't such a tough life after all. I'm sorry that maybe I didn't (always) act like a lady about the whole thing." And, concludes: "I'm a black woman. I'm not alone. I'm free and no longer have to be a symbol to anybody. I'm me—like nobody else."

For smooth listening, get a copy of Lena's *We'll Be Together Again* and *An Evening with Lena* 1993 and '94 albums on CD. You will play them forever and ever.

I have just received my invitation to be present at a Society of Singers tribute to Lena Horne in late June, 1997, at Avery Fisher Hall, Lincoln Center, New York It will be a great party for a great Song Star. It will also be a celebration of Lena's 80th birthday.

Benny Goodman and Frances Langford 1937.
(Jack Ellsworth Collection)

FRANCES LANGFORD

Where There's Hope, There's Langford.

In 1993 I sent Frances Langford a letter along with a copy of an article I had written for *World War II* Magazine about her old boss Bob Hope and their wartime travels with the USO. Everyone knows that Frances, whom Bob dubbed "Mother Langford" on those trips because of the concerned motherly nurturing of some of the troupers, was one of the original entertainers engaged by Bob to help entertain our servicemen during the dark days of that terrible war. Frances responded from her Florida residence with a kind reply inviting me to interview her. Before I could reach for the phone, I misplaced the telephone number and lost my chance.

Then in 1995, as I embarked upon this book, my intense search for data about the Song Stars turned up the missing letter intact with the phone number. My call to Frances was welcomed. Frances' only contact with her contemporaries these days is limited to periodical conversations with Bob Hope and limited appearances, mostly for benefits. After some words about mutual friends Connie Haines and Kitty Kallen, we reminisced about the life of Song Star Frances Langford.

Born in Lakeland, Florida, in 1914, Frances studied opera at Southern College, but tonsillitis altered her vocal capacity from soprano to contralto. "I was very surprised at the change in my own voice," she said, "it was like listening to someone else."

Band singer and radio star Rudy Vallee heard her sing in New Orleans in 1935 and invited her to appear on his radio show *Rudy Vallee and His Connecticut Yankees*. She practiced her singing skills on Rudy's show for over a year.

A role in the unsuccessful New York stage play, *Here Goes the Bride* in 1933 was devastating to her career. However, at Cole Porter's birthday party held atop the Waldorf Astoria in New York, she sang *Night and Day*, which was then Cole's newest song. This was before Fred Astaire and Ginger Rogers put the song to work in the movies, and long before Frank Sinatra recorded the definitive version.

"Johnny Green was the orchestra leader. Cole asked me to sing his song *Night and Day* at his party. I rehearsed it briefly and then sang it....I believe...the first public performance of the song. Many important show business people was there including movie producer Walter Wanger. That night he invited me out to Hollywood for a screen test. I did my first picture for him."

This led to a part in *Every Night at Eight* with George Raft and the movie *Collegiate*, both in 1935. They were followed by *Broadway Melody of 1936; Hollywood Hotel* in 1937 (with Benny Goodman and his orchestra who was very hot at this point); *Too Many Girls* in 1940, and *Hit Parade of 1941*. In 1939 Frances was chosen as The All-American Girl.

A radio role was created for her on *Hollywood Hotel*, an hour-long popular weekly variety show with Hollywood actor Dick Powell as Master-of-Ceremonies. The program featured a twenty-minute dramatic production with Hollywood stars, introduced by celebrated gossip columnist Louella Parsons.

Within a few years, Frances Langford had shared the mike with just about every important vocalist of the time: Louis Armstrong (*Pennies from Heaven*-also with Bing), Rudy Vallee, Tony Martin, Bob Hope, and Bing Crosby (*Gypsy Love Song* which illustrates the sweet capable voice that was early Frances working with Bing's rich baritone). Frances also worked her pipes with the Jimmy Dorsey, Benny Goodman, Skinnay Ennis, Stan Kenton, and the Les Brown Bands. "That's pretty good credentials, isn't it Richard?" "Are you kidding?" said I.

Remember James Cagney's wonderful 1942 film *Yankee Doodle Dandy*? Well, it was Frances Langford who vocalized the thrilling version of George M. Cohan's song *Over There*. That's my overall favorite Frances Langford performance. She belted, she delivered it with an enthusiasm unlike anyone else.

"Jimmy (Cagney) called me and wanted me to do those (George M.) Cohan numbers because he said I would do them better than any-

Frances Langford on a USO Tour in Algiers in 1942 with L to R: Bob Hope, Tony Romano and Jerry Colonna. (Courtesy USO)

one else. I was very pleased—it was a big and wonderful film....and it's lasted so long. I see it on television every now and then." To me Frances sounded proud of that achievement.

During her travels with Bob Hope, she performed personally for and was befriended by generals Jimmy Doolittle, George Patton, and Dwight Eisenhower while overseas on those USO tours. General Eisenhower decorated Frances with a special citation for unselfishly entertaining our troops under wartime conditions.

There was a charming story about Frances' first experience singing to Naval personnel at the San Diego, California Naval Base. "It seems they had to cut the song *You Go to My Head*, realizing a little late that the word *head* was the Navy word for toilet." she told me to giggles.

Servicemen, especially overseas, always enjoyed Frances Langford, usually the first American girl seen by them in months. When she would sing a sentimental ballad, some of them would actually shed tears. Seeing a very pretty all-American girl from home and listening to familiar songs they associated with their own sweethearts brought back visions of home that jokes alone could not achieve, even when delivered by a great comic like Bob Hope.

As Bob Hope recounted to me during one of our interviews: "...I'll always love the ones with heart and courage who went with me on USO tours during the war, like Frances Langford. I couldn't have done it without her and the others," a great acknowledgment of her talents and character, indeed! Frances traversed the entire war zone with Bob during all those courageous trips.

"We started in Alaska...doing little shows in quonset huts of less than a hundred people...Alaska was a foreign country then," Frances explained, "..and then in so many other camps all around the country. Tony Romano (guitarist) and Jerry (Colonna-comedian) were always with us as was dancer Patty Thomas and sometimes song-and-dance man Jack Pepper. Bob called us his fearless gypsies. Then we went to England and the other British Isles and then to Africa. It was always great fun. Bob was always funnier offstage than onstage. He's a great man. Just like an everyday person."

By 1945, the war over, Frances starred on her own radio show back home, so she had to quit the tours. Frances was inadvertently responsible for Bob Hope's long association with Les Brown and his Orchestra. It seems that in 1948 Bob was searching for a replacement for Frances, who had been with him on his radio show for years, and someone brought him records of Les Brown and his singer Doris Day. Doris never joined the show, but Bob was so enamored by the sounds of Les Brown that he signed up him and his orchestra. They remain together even today.

In 1952 I was working the Martin & Lewis telethon at the NBC studios in New York. That's where I first met Frances Langford and Tony Romano. My job was to cue them onstage at the right time. We shared a sandwich at noon and talked about, what else, those USO tours. She appeared onstage exactly at 1:19 AM right after Phil Silvers and Jerry Lester.

In 1953 Frances Langford appeared briefly in the movie *The Glenn Miller Story* which starred June Allyson and Jimmy Stewart. She played along with performers Louis Armstrong, Gene Krupa, bandleader Ben Pollack, and Glenn's regular singing group The Modernaires, all playing themselves. Frances sang a great rendition of the first gold record ever, Chattanogga Choo-Choo with Glenn and the Modernaires near the end of the movie.

In 1959, Frances and Ralph Evinrude married, and Bob was able to convince Ralph to allow Frances to perform once again with Bob and his traveling Christmas USO troupe consisting of the old World War II cast: guitarist Tony Romano, dancer Patty Thomas, and Bob's old sidekick, comedian Jerry Colonna. Ralph also went along for the ride. Movie stars Jayne Mansfield and Steve McQueen also joined that tour begun at Alaska's Ladd Air Force Base and continued appearances at other nearby, northern bases, bringing *home* to servicemen at lonely outposts during Christmastime.

Then, there's the saga of the *Bickerson's*, the long-running, outrageous weekly radio show aired in the mid-fifties and ran into the '70's. Don Ameche was *John* and Frances Langford played *Blanche*. They screamed fiercely at one another every week over the radio. Blanche would accuse John; John would fight back; then Blanche would cry, and John would repent. It was the marriage experience portrayed at its worst. The hilarious show lasted for a number of years.

127

"They even made two albums of the show and they sold pretty good," Frances said.

On the *Hollywood Palace*, a television variety show, Frances appeared with her friend Bing Crosby, along with old pal Don Ameche and the King Family in April of 1967. The year 1991 had her appearing with a long list of other stars on a television show called *Stars and Stripes*, depicting Hollywood and World War II American movie classics. Tony Randall narrated while Maxene Andrews of the Andrews Sisters, Dorothy Lamour, Eddie Bracken, Bob Hope, and Bing Crosby performed in clips covering performances at military camps and their selling of war bonds.

To list the recordings of Frances Langford would take too many pages. Her work has been accompanied by everyone from Jesse Crawford's great organ to the fine orchestra of Victor Young. She has sung duets with Tony Martin and Bing Crosby. She has done it all. She has done it well.

"What are you doing for fun these days?"

"Well, you won't believe it..." she was filled with pride, "I am a deep-sea fisherman."

"A what?" I shot back to this petite, retired Florida citizen.

"My biggest catch was a 750 pound blue-fin tuna."

"HOLY SMOKES......how do you do that? How does anyone do that?"

"I've always been a fisherman...for years. I just know how to do it. You have to know how," she re-assured me. "We have a 110 foot boat, the *Santa Clare*. Me and my husband have taken the boat to Europe and fish all the way." Her husband is Mr. Stuart, former Secretary of the Air Force under Roosevelt during World War II and now a Tulsa, Oklahoma, attorney.

Frances is an admirer of Peggy Lee, "She's the best of everybody when it comes to singing." She also likes Connie Haines, "She's so cute." She holds great affection for Kitty Kallen, Jo Stafford, and Keely Smith. "I think Keely is fabulous. Great voice."

Frances also counted Bing Crosby among her friends, "He was so sweet. I was always around him quite a bit because of Bob. It was always lots of fun being around the two of them." Frances performed with Bob recently in Lakeland, Florida, and Milwaukee, Wisconsin, at charity shows. They keep in touch.

But, she went on, "I don't see anybody much anymore, I'm away from all that...you know..living in Florida. I don't go to those parties like I used to."

Not too many of us will forget the face and voice of the lovely Frances Langford, all-American girl and absolute Song Star.

Jo Stafford sent us this photo of her singing *You Belong to Me*.
(Jo Stafford Collection)

JO STAFFORD

The Stafford Sisters Lead Singer Goes Solo

There's a record and tape marketer who lists the albums of Song Star Jo Stafford on a "last chance to buy page," always stating: "Supplies are limited for this music treasury. Inventories are low and when they're gone, there'll be no more. So don't miss out. Order yours today!" Well, they have been hawking that old hat trick for thirty years. When Jo's songs *You Belong to Me, Long Ago and Far Away, My Darling, My Darling, I'll Be Seeing You, You'll Never Know, There Are Such Things,* and *Embraceable You* stop selling, the Earth will surely stop spinning.

Jo Stafford and her songs are at the very root of America's musical legacy. To the G.I.'s of World War II, she was *G.I.Jo* because of her association with those stirring, ever-familiar strains our servicemen, known as G.I.'s (Government Issue), clung to during those desperate wartime days. It has been said that when men go to war they need a connection to home. Jo Stafford reminded them of "home." Her voice evoked calm and reassurance when it was needed most. Jo seemed to be the clean cut—not the pin-up, type, but the wholesome high school sweetheart. Her recordings touched them in barracks, field kitchens and hospitals. When she sang *I'll Be Seeing You* or *There Are Such Things*, memories began and comfort was felt.

Jo Stafford started with a singing group composed of her own two sisters and herself. "We were known as the Stafford Sisters," she explained. "By the age of ten, I was reading music and could play piano pretty good." Sisters Pauline and Christine were older and first performed as a duet on Long Beach, California, radio station KFOX with their own show. "I was able to join up with them upon graduation from high school," she added as we spoke across three thousand miles of telephone wire, her in springlike California and me on win-

131

try Long Island. That re-assuring, instantly recognizable smoothness materialized beautifully over those wires, sounding precisely as it always has all these years and on every recording she has ever made.

"It was the very natural thing to do," she said, "and we had quite a successful run of it." The trio worked the southern California radio circuit and backed up Hollywood movie musicals. Earlier, Jo had received several years of classical voice training, with an eye to some day becoming an opera singer. That never materialized. "I simply had to go to work after high school."

Then, in 1938, Jo joined up with a group of seven men singers, calling themselves The Pied Pipers. "I graduated to the Pipers and we worked on the movie called *Alexander's Ragtime Band* (an Irving Berlin musical starring Alice Faye, Tyrone Power, and Don Ameche). The Pipers were literally born on the set between takes when we started to sing together. We would sit on the studio floor and work out parts of a song."

The Pipers joined up with the Tommy Dorsey aggregation in 1938, but after a while Tommy realized he could not afford to pay all eight, so he let them go. When the group reduced itself to four members (Chuck Lowrey, Clark Yocum, John Huddleston, and Jo), Tommy re-hired them in December of 1939 and added a skinny kid named Frank Sinatra as the regular band singer. They went on to record a batch of very successful hits: *There Are Such Things, Street of Dreams, Oh, Look at Me Now* (the latter with Connie Haines) and the biggest hit of all, the one that established vocal groups forever, *I'll Never Smile Again.*

Jo Stafford remembered Frank Sinatra when he first joined the band and the Pipers, "As he came up to the mike, I just thought, Hmmm—kinda thin. But by the end of eight bars I was thinking, 'This is the greatest sound I've ever heard.' But he had more. Call it talent. You knew he couldn't do a number badly."

Jo was the Pied Pipers' lead singer and a regularly featured soloist with Dorsey, but, "I always considered myself, first and foremost, the distaff member of the Pied Pipers." Jo was considered an especially cool, self-assured person with great musical control and a sly equally cool sense of humor. She was loved by everyone in the organization. She soon began singing solo ballads. It was Connie

Jo Stafford 1944.
(Courtesy Capitol Records)

Haines who sang the cutesy, upbeat numbers. Connie told me that Tommy Dorsey called Jo "....the mellow trombone voice of the band."

In 1943, utilizing her talents and armed with techniques learned from Tommy Dorsey's trombone playing, the endearing Jo Stafford left the Pipers, and, at the request of her friend, Dorsey junkie and prolific composer-songwriter Johnny Mercer, began recording for the newly formed Capitol Records out in California.

Just when Jo Stafford and the Pipers began with Dorsey, her future husband, arranger Paul Weston, had left the band to oversee the musical career of Dinah Shore, write music charts for the Bob Crosby Band, and also to work for Paramount Pictures on Hope and Crosby road films. He had written two big songs that Sinatra and others including Jo recorded, *I Should Care* and *Day by Day*.

Paul Weston was Johnny Mercer's first musical director at Capitol and was the influence and arranger of many of Jo's hits such as *Whispering Hope* and *My Darling, My Darling*, duets with baritone Gordon MacRae. *Whispering* still sells well, but mostly in the southern part of the country. Jo recorded many first-class hits with Johnny. *Candy* in 1945 with John and the Pipers, *Long Ago and Far Away* and *I Love You*. She was one of the first popular singers to record folk songs and novelties: *Feudin' and Fightin'* and *I'm My Own Grandmaw'*.

After twelve years of working together at Capitol, and subsequently at Columbia, where she recorded the hits *You Belong to Me*, *Shrimp Boats* (written by Paul himself), *Make Love to Me*, and *Jambalaya* (written by the great Hank Williams, Sr.), Jo Stafford and Paul Weston married in 1952. It wasn't unusual that singers and musicians married. Doris Day married Les Brown saxist George Weidner; Peggy Lee married Goodman guitarist Dave Barbour; Frances Wayne married Woody Herman trumpeter Neal Hefti; June Christy married Stan Kenton tenor saxist Bob Cooper; June Hutton (who replaced Jo in the Pipers) married Axel Stordahl (Tommy Dorsey and Frank Sinatra arranger), and Kitty Kallen's first marraige was to a Jack Teagarden clarinet player. Some singers married their bosses: Harriet Hilliard married Ozzie Nelson, Georgia Carroll married Kay Kyser,

Dorothy Collins married Raymond Scott, Ann Richards married Stan Kenton, and Betty Grable married Harry James.

"Paul and I produced albums of parodied, off-keyed music under the pseudonym Jonathan and Darlene Edwards, just for the fun of it, which included drummer Jack Sperling (who had to quit because he couldn't stop laughing). It was sort of a musical joke, where Paul played piano and I would sing, well, with too many beats to the bar and with wrong chords, perhaps characterized as a slightly inebriated duet—all for fun. We never thought it could catch on." A handful of albums were sustained and actually sold well, and the strange duet remarkably developed a loyal following. They were the alter-ego of an otherwise more serious, but rather dull, pair of musicians. You can find those two silly performers doing the Darlene and Jonathan thing on their own label, Corinthian Records.

Jo and Paul Weston spent the summer of 1961 in London doing a set of television shows. They became as equally endeared to the British population as they had to their fans in their own country.

It is safe to say, and by her own admission, that Jo Stafford never enjoyed performing before an audience and never craved stardom. She much preferred the recording studio and was immensely successful in the process. During the period of her reign, 1939 through the middle-sixties, Jo Stafford was always in the top five when it came to popularity polls and almost always the number one girl vocalist. When her record sales with Columbia reached twenty-five million in 1954, they presented her with a Diamond Award.

Now, you would think such an illustrious and prolific performer would want her career to climb even higher but, instead, Jo Stafford's singing career came to a grinding halt. Why? Because her children's welfare was more important to her than a celebrity singing career, so she gave it all up. She didn't want her children Tim and Amy to have to confront the adversarial challenges most children of entertainers in that part of the world seem to face. She feared the possibilities of drugs, the disruptive behavior spawned by parental neglect, and loneliness produced in adolescents by parents touring, albeit missing parents. Jo Stafford's judgment proved true, as borne out by the known debris left behind by other celebrities who shared the same problem,

135

but, maybe after some consideration, chose different roads than the Weston's.

From Jo Stafford's first solo recording, *Little Man With A Candy Cigar*, to her parodies as Darlene Edwards, she has proved that a successful career and a successful home life can be achieved if it is desired. Now, Jo Stafford, with Paul gone, sings only for her grandchildren (2 grandsons and 2 granddaughters) and spends her life in her comfortable Century City, California, home. Her son has his own recording company and her daughter is currently singing with a Big Band.

For Jo Stafford, the apples surely do happily fall close to the tree. Her instincts were right on target. This is what she worked so hard for all those years.

Jo was delighted to discover that her recording of *You Belong to Me* made the 60 year all-time listeners list of favorite songs polled in 1997 by New York's favorite radio station for American standards, WQEW. Nice job, Jo.

"Nice job WQEW, and nice job Richard—and thanks for remembering me to everyone." The photo for this chapter was chosen by Jo herself. You will notice she is singing.

Tommy Dorsey Orchestra 1941. L to R (top row): Pied Pipers, Chuck Lowrey, Jo Stafford and John Huddleston. Also girl singer Connie Haines and boy singer Frank Sinatra; and below, drummer Buddy Rich.

Anita O'Day in 1941.
(Courtesy Alan Eichler)

ANITA O'DAY

A New Era in Jazz Singing Begins

When former dancer Anita O'Day joined the Gene Krupa Band in 1941, an entirely new era in jazz vocalizing was officially launched. This girl had a definite personality and set a style of band singing that dominated the 1940's.

"She was a wild chick, all right," her new boss recalled, "but, boy, how she could sing." Unlike the feminine, cute, little-girl presence of her counterparts, Anita scored as a hip jazz musician. Even her clothes were different, looking more like the musicians' attire, than girl singer tresses and ribbons. It was take-me-as-I am-or-get-out-of-my-way style.

Drummer Gene promptly teamed Anita up with another new talented acquisition, a small guy nick-named "Little Jazz," electrifying trumpeter Roy Eldridge. Roy had an already established reputation in jazz improvisation, between them a creative new swinging musical style fully blossomed. The co-mingling of instrument and voice-instrument worked well. The band flourished with *Let Me Off Uptown* (her best performance with Krupa for my money), *Georgia on My Mind, Green Eyes* and *Murder He Says*, where, as Roy said, "Anita sounds like a jazz horn." Anita herself declares her unusual, husky voice was the result of a tonsillectomy that went partially wrong. It forced her to sing in short phrases. They recorded many exciting sides together, but the alliance of vocalist and soloist didn't last very long. The relationship broke down between them and a feud actually developed. Fortunately, those innovative recordings still hold up very well today. Thanks to Anita O'Day, it was Krupa's best years as a bandleader.

Critics of the time said Anita had more in common with Song Star Billie Holiday than Billie's contemporary counterpart Ella Fitzgerald. Teddy Wilson told me that at one time he couldn't tell Bil-

139

lie from Anita on certain songs. Anita delivered those long-held feathery notes, bending an occasional tone like Billie, so that the combined effect was a gathering of unmistakable, rhythmic jazz material never quite heard that way. For sure, a composite of Billie and Ella with shades of Bessie. And, why not! They were the obvious influences of Anita's early musical experiences.

A jazz singer, by definition, works in an instrumental manner, improvising just like a musician does on his instrument. In the case of Anita O'Day, she has always been able to do just that: altering the tune as the song progresses, creating interesting melody lines— short of "scatting." That's what Billie did!

So, a jazz singer's voice is much like a musician's instrument. The voice improvises while it provides vocals and sounds, like "scat" singing in the style of Ella, Armstrong, early Crosby, or super-scat Mel Torme'. When Anita turned her efforts to ballads, she offered a very different voice and interpretation. She could be sensitive and subdued, unlike her usual hip, swinging style. Words were unimportant-interpretation was paramount. For Anita it was expression in a new abstract mode.

In the spring of 1944, Anita linked up with band leader Stan Kenton, commencing the band's swingingest history. She motivated the band with her direct, swinging singing style. The masterful tenor sax of Stan Getz and the arrangements of Dave Matthews (who also played tenor sax) moved the band with infectious numbers, including Anita's impeccable 1944 version of *And Her Tears Flowed Like Wine* (my personal O'Day favorite—so much a definitive jazz classic) recorded that May. Anita stayed with the band for just a short time.

This new school of singing ushered in by Anita O'Day had its roots in early jazz vocalizing and its torch was passed on to the singers who immediately followed her. It was June Christy in 1945 who followed Anita in the Stan Kenton organization and continued the style. Anita had actually found Shirley Luster (later known as June Christy) singing at the Three Deuces Club in Chicago and told her she was leaving Kenton. She advised June to apply for the job. Anita had become very tired, almost unable to keep up with the demanding nightly "gigs."

Un-importantly, Anita sang briefly for Benny Goodman in 1943 and joined in another association in October, 1959, when Benny put together a group fronted by xylophonist Red Norvo and hired Anita to sing for the group. The tour covered much of Europe and lasted one month. According to Anita, Benny continually upstaged her, as he was known to do to his vocalists.

"Benny didn't want anyone to stand out above him or his orchestra," she said, "and a few days into the tour, he cut me down to just two numbers." Goodman was accused by others of blatantly attempting to monopolize the spotlight during performances.

The Man I Love, recorded in 1954, is where Anita O'Day shows her stuff—stretching notes, bending them and bringing them back, recreating melody as she moves along and spontaneously reconstructing melodies while in musical flight. She "scat" the lyrics like the be-bopper she was becoming.

In 1956, Anita O'Day recorded *Honeysuckle Rose* and *The Nightingale Sang in Berkeley Square.* Oh!, how I love that recording of *Nightingale*. The huskiness in her voice is deep and prominent, the mood elegant and even sexy. It is a classy little-known gem recorded earlier by Bing Crosby in December of 1940. I consider it to be one of Anita's best ever recordings. It's timbre and richness, backed up with strings and a Corky Hale harp in this full version, almost outshines Bing's noble and meritorious efforts. Her voice is the equivalent of a low group of harmonious instruments rising and increasing with the fullness of the piece as demanded, as though carefully measured instruments were subjoined and then taken away. It's downright beautiful to hear over and over again. Anita is performing it again—right now—for me, while I write about her unique career. In the 1982 version of the *Jazz Book,* author Joachim Berendt declared Anita O'Day to be "the greatest white female jazz vocalist, with, if I may add, musical assurance of virtuoso caliber and great improvisational capacity."

During the 1970's Anita played regularly at Ye Little Club in Beverly Hills and occasionally returned to engagements at Reno Sweeney's showcase in New York City. Anita was also part entrepreneur, selling record albums at the gate at retail prices instead of marketing them through normal distribution channels. Of course, it kept the albums from garnishing the deserved attention by critics and distributors it would have ordinarily received.

In March of 1980, Anita hooked up with a Mel Torme' show at Carnegie Hall called Mel Torme' and Friends that also featured Woody Herman and his Herd, saxophonist Jerry Mulligan, and pianists Teddy Wilson, Bill Evans and George Shearing. As Mel punctuated in his book *It Wasn't All Velvet*, "What friends!"

In her biography *Hard Times, High Times*, Anita told her life's story with no punches pulled. She tells it pretty much the way she sings and performs. Everyone realizes that *you always know what you get* from Anita O'Day. Frankie Laine proves the point in his biographical book *That Lucky Old Son*: "In 1935, before I left the Arcadia Ballroom (Elizabeth, New Jersey), I became acquainted with a precocious little girl in the marathon dancing contest who was already developing into a mature vocalist at the age of 14. She would follow me around like a little puppy after every song I sang and pepper me with questions: 'Why did you pick that tune? Why did you phrase like that? How come....how come....how come?' Of course, when they found out she was underage they pulled her right off the floor, but her brief stint in the contest marked the beginning of my association with a lady who became one of our great jazz stylists, Anita O'Day."

Anita went on the quest for learning her craft during those early years, sitting in at various musicians' haunts in Chicago until someone would hire her to sing. She had just changed her name to *O'Day* from *Colton* before Gene Krupa caught her one night during a club date. He listened to her sing but one song and hired her.

Some years ago actress Jane Fonda was supposed to re-create Anita in a movie about her life, but it never materialized. Lately, Dennis Hopper, the actor, was supposed to buy the rights for such a movie, but I understand the deal recently fell through, or at least it was placed on hold.

Anita O'Day still sings today, but on a limited basis. In 1994 she performed at the Sportsman Lodge in Studio City, California, for the Society of Singers Ladies Who Sang with the Bands benefit. The song was *Let Me Off Uptown* with the band trumpeter doing the Roy Eldridge part.

Anita O'Day today.
(Courtesy Alan Eichler)

As Yankees great Yoga Berra once declared, "It was *deja vu* all over again."

Anita is having a tough time these days due to falling from her bike and fracturing her right arm. She is now receiving physical therapy to help restore its use. While in the hospital she was honored with an American Jazz Masters Fellowship which enriched her by $20,000.00.

Discover O'Day today. Listen to the cute and wordy ditty *Massachusetts* and the hip *Opus No. 1*. They will tell the story. You'll find yourself searching for O'Day everywhere.

Jack Ellsworth reminded me of a set of Cole Porter lyrics once sang by Anita O'Day on a Verve recording of *You're the Top* that punctuates the quality of our unique Song Star, Anita O'Day:

You're the *bop*, you're like Sarah singin'
You're the *bop*, you're like Yardbird swingin'
You're the minus gong, you're the greatest song
that Eckstine ever sung,
You're a Moscow mule, you're so cool
You're Lester Young
You're the high in a *Downbeat* tally,
You're the guy who owns Tin Pan Alley
You're Tatum's left hand, a Goodman swing band,
A Lena Horne who won't stop
But if baby I'm the bottom, you're the *bop*!

144

Dolly Dawn sketch by Leroy Neiman. 1978.
(Courtesy Dolly Dawn)

Goodman, Krupa, Dawn Win O. W. Awards

Honored As Year's Outstanding Stars

THE 1937 ORCHESTRA WORLD ACHIEVEMENT AWARD closed on January 17, 1938, elevating Benny Goodman, orchestra leader; Gene Krupa, musician; and Dolly Dawn, orchestra vocalist into the three top ranks of selection. According to the thousands who participated in this first annual poll, Goodman, Krupa, and Dawn are the outstanding individuals in the music business for the year 1937.

Taking an early lead, the leaders maintained their position throughout the entire poll. All were selected by overwhelming majorities, ranging nearly 50% ahead of their nearest competitors.

The rise of Martha Tilton as an orchestra vocalist is amazing. Only a few months in the business, she copped second place in a field of nearly 60 vocalists.

Dorsey Strong

Equally interesting is the fact that Tommy Dorsey, more so than Benny Goodman, is regarded as a leader close to his instrument. Tommy polled second place both in the orchestra leader and musician columns.

The ACHIEVEMENT AWARD is the mark of achievement set up by THE ORCHESTRA WORLD to recognize the leader, the musician, and the vocalist who accomplished the most benefit for the music business during the year. It was not a popularity contest.

From the field of hundreds of entries the following are the 20 readers in all three groups.

Orchestra Leader
1. BENNY GOODMAN
2. TOMMY DORSEY
3. BOB CROSBY
4. Jimmie Lunceford
5. Horace Heidt
6. Hal Kemp
7. Casa Loma
8. Bunny Berigan
9. Raymond Scott
10. Duke Ellington
11. Jimmy Dorsey
12. Art Shaw
13. Woody Herman
14. Chick Webb
15. Guy Lombardo
16. Eddy Duchin
17. Fletcher Henderson
18. Hudson-DeLange
19. Red Norvo
20. Sammy Kaye

Musician
1. GENE KRUPA
2. TOMMY DORSEY
3. HARRY JAMES
4. Benny Goodman
5. Ray Bauduc
6. Teddy Wilson
7. Lionel Hampton
8. Louis Armstrong
9. Bunny Berigan
10. Artie Shaw
11. Adrian Rollini
12. Art Tatum
13. Johnny Hodges
14. Ray McKinley

THE ORCHESTRA WORLD
Achievement Award
WINNERS FOR 1937
Leader
BENNY GOODMAN
Musician
GENE KRUPA
Orchestra Vocalist
DOLLY DAWN

BENNY GOODMAN
1937's Outstanding Leader

GENE KRUPA
1937's Outstanding Musician

DOLLY DAWN
1937's Outstanding Vocalist

15. Bob Zerke
16. Jack Teagarden
17. "Red" Norvo
18. "Fats" Waller
19. Jimmy Dorsey
20. Coleman Hawkins

Orchestra Vocalist
1. DOLLY DAWN
2. MARTHA TILTON
3. JACK LEONARD
4. Edythe Wright
5. Mildred Bailey
6. Ella Fitzgerald
7. Kay Weber
8. Kenny Sargent
9. Connie Boswell
10. Ivy Anderson
11. Maxine Sullivan
12. "Pee Wee" Hunt
13. Perry Como
14. Louis Armstrong
15. Billie Halliday
16. Maxine
17. Peg LaCentra
18. Maxine Grey
19. Skinny Ennis
20. Helen Ward

The contest brought selections from every part of the United States; from Canada, Mexico, Philippine Islands, Alaska, Great Britain, Australia, South Africa, India, France, Denmark, Hawaii, South America—and one coupon from Japan.

Radio Eds Vote

Included in the final returns are the selections of nearly two hundred radio editors of the United States, who were canvassed in a special sub-poll. It is interesting to note that their selections coincided with the three final selections, but were at complete variance with the rest of the leaders. Few got past Gene Krupa in selections for the musician's award. Benny Goodman and Dolly Dawn were overwhelming choices for orchestra leader and vocalist.

In recognition of their selections, Goodman, Krupa, and Dawn will be presented with plaques, commemorating their 1937 achievement. It is expected that these plaques will be awarded on radio programs featuring these artists. Plans for the presentation were being made as THE ORCHESTRA WORLD went to press.

The "Orchestra World" Survey declares Dolly Dawn #1 Vocalist. February 1938. (Dolly Dawn Collection)

146

DOLLY DAWN

Remembering the Dawn Patrol

Dolly Dawn, personable, prolific, rhythmic recording star of the '30's and '40's, and I talked ourselves "blue" one night in January 1997 at her New York City apartment. At home earlier, I played some of Dolly's old tunes: *Summertime* (shades of Mildred Bailey, Doris Day and Connee Boswell are there), which she does so beautifully, clearly, artfully, with great feeling; the unforgettable *It's a Sin to Tell a Lie* -so sincere, and *I Stumbled Over Love*. Dolly's friend, press agent and New York Sheet Music Society Secretary Anthony DiFlorio III, introduced me to the very gentle lady who was first showcased in George Hall's band on the radio from the Grill Room at New York's Hotel Taft precisely on May 30, 1935. That relationship lasted until 1941, according to Dolly.

Dolly Dawn was one of the quiet giants of the Big Band Era. Born Teresa Anna Marie Stabile: "I was only nine when I began singing in Newark, New Jersey, on a Saturday morning radio show, accompanied by another unknown youngster, guitarist Tony Mottola." Dubbed *Billie Star* she would eventually be christened *Dolly Dawn* (a name she never been comfortable with) at the age of fourteen: "She's dimpled like a doll and as fresh and lovely as the dawn," declared *Journal-American* radio columnist Harriet Menchen at a dinner one night with young Teresa and her parents while searching for a stage name for the young singer. Hence, the sobriquet *Dolly Dawn*.

Dolly had won a contest at the Loew's State Theater in Newark at age eleven. At thirteen she auditioned for George Hall's band, reminded him of the contest she had won and got the job...and kept it. "This was precisely on May 30, 1935." Dolly recalled.

After six years, Hall actually turned the band over to his very popular singer, now the band's strongest attraction. On the night of

July 4, 1941, at a ceremony at New York's Roseland Ballroom on Broadway, she was named the band's new leader as well as lead singer. From then on it was "Dolly Dawn and Her Dawn Patrol."

Hall remained manager and had to be designated Dolly's legal guardian in order to allow her to appear publicly at such a young age in places where liquor was being served. Hall and his wife performed the paperwork and, unknown to Dolly, kept her from invitations to appear in movies, on Broadway, and quashed potential deals with other bands:

"Tommy Dorsey called me and invited me to sing with his band and I automatically turned the call over to George Hall who, unbeknown to me, squashed the deal. I didn't realize then the damage he had done to my career over a short period of time when I was in demand."

The Dorsey band was the springboard of many a great star. By virtue of her performances with the band, Dolly became Hall's meal ticket: "..... and so he kept me from every opportunity—but I did not know this until many years after he passed on, when a friend and former MCA band booker revealed it all to me once during a dinner party. I trusted Hall completely as did my parents whom he was paying five-hundred each week, but he did not take care of me financially. At the end there was no money, and he didn't even make any Social Security payments to insure my future." Dolly received no royalties from her recordings, much like many other Song Stars. Ironically, when George Hall became ill, Dolly dutifully took care of him until his death in 1963.

"I renamed the band 'Dolly Dawn and The Dawn Patrol,' " she said, "after Ed Sullivan's New York daily newspaper column 'Along The Dawn Patrol.' " The group was composed of Dolly and seven musicians. Her personal best: "*It's a Sin to Tell a Lie,* written by wonderful Fats Waller himself."

Some of Dolly's other recording successes were *Every Minute of the Hour*; *Oh! Ma-Ma* (The Butcher Boy-an immensely popular song of the late thirties); *You're a Sweetheart*, which reached No. 1; *I'll Stand By*, and *Pig Foot Pete*. She composed *The Little Birdies* and *Keep Dreaming*. Her recording of *Beethoven Wrote It but, It Swings* in 1939 is simply terrific. The band broke up when they ran out of musicians to play because of World War II. "We were constantly rehearsing with new guys. It became impossible to continue," she explained. She embarked on a solo career, playing clubs and theaters. She made an album in 1982 and her recording of *It's a Sin to Tell a Lie* became the background for Steve Martin's film *Pennies from Heaven* and was reissued on the soundtrack album.

Dolly was an early friend of Song Star Ella Fitzgerald. When Ella first started out she placed a telephone call to Dolly after constantly listening to her sing over the radio. "I invited her to my hotel," Dolly told me, "When she arrived, she said, 'I'm Ella Fitzgerald and I want to be a singer just like you.' So I greeted her and we talked quite a bit and I told her how I learned to sing. I encouraged her to continue to try her luck. She was a sweet girl and, as a result of that first meeting, we became lifelong friends." A few years ago, when Ella was performing at Avery Fisher Hall in New York, she invited Dolly to a performance and then backstage where the two resumed their old friendship. The two stars had admired one another as their careers paralleled through the years, Ella wishing she could sing sweet ballads like Dolly and Dolly wishing she could "scat" sing like Ella.

Dolly also acknowledges her debt to Connee Boswell and Mildred Bailey, "who paved the way for all of us," she explained.

Anthony Di Florio III strongly feels that Dolly is one of the most underrated singers. Anthony regularly writes about Dolly declaring that she was actually one of the most influential singing stars of the Swing Era. "She was a symbol of that golden age of popular songs— the songs our people love to perform and collect," he said, "Dolly introduced hundreds of those songs on radio and records in the thirties and forties. We'll all feel lucky when some of those great performances are finally re-issued on CDs!"

Reviewing Dolly's 1989 *Memories of You* album featuring pianist Tony Monte, bassist Milt Hinton, guitarist Bucky Pizzerelli, bassist George Duvivier, bassist Butch Miles, reed player Phil Bodner, and guitarist Gene Bertoncini, Rex Reed said "Dolly Dawn makes a room glow with warmth and love," and *The New York Times'* John S. Wilson stated "...she has an effortless way of finding just the right groove for her songs, whether she is being a torch singer, putting a perceptive life in her phrasing as she swings, or implying rhythmic momen-

149

**Dolly Dawn and "Memories of You" composer Eubie Blake.
(Dolly Dawn Collection)**

tum in a slow ballad." Those are credentials for greatness. The album was masterfully engineered and arranged by Tony Monte.

Recently, Dolly Dawn was the subject of a three-hour WQEW, Rich Conaty *Big Broadcast* program sponsored by Mutual Of America and held at their "Nightclub" atop 320 Park Avenue in New York City. It was taped and made into a video. Rich is an old friend of mine from his Fordham radio station days, when I was with Long Island PM magazine and we helped one another. He's still a very young man who is committed to the preservation of the music and entertainment heritage of the Jazz Age.

"My best moments have been all of them-every bit of it," Dolly responded blithely to my last inquiry. As to her favorites: "Peggy Lee is a terrific singer. I always admired Helen Ward and Jo Stafford, and my all time favorite is Helen Forrest."

It's easy to make a friend of Dolly Dawn. She's just that kind of Song Star. Last week I sent Dolly a porcelain doll from my wife Jeanette's Doll Shop. It reminded me of Dolly Dawn. When she received it, she wholeheartedly agreed.

My favorite inscribed Patti Page photo 1965.
(Richard Grudens Collection)

PATTI PAGE

Clara Ann (Katy) Fowler, Tenth of Eleven

One of my all-time favorite recordings of any era is Katy Fowler's rendition of a song titled *Old Cape Cod*. Katy, born in Claremore, Oklahoma, in 1927, the tenth of eleven children, became forever known as Patti Page after filling in for an anonymous singing star of a Tulsa radio show *Meet Patti Page*, sponsored by a local dairy, the Page Milk Company. She sounded as good to me on *Old Cape Cod* as she did earlier to Jack Rael, who, traveling through Tulsa, Oklahoma, heard her and offered to become her manager.

"She accepted my offer and we became a partnership that has to be the longest-lasting show business relationship in history," Jack said to me as we sat and talked about Patti's career, "...it lasted for fifty years...as of last October." As author Arnold Shaw stated in his biography of Harry Belafonte, entitled *Belafonte,* "There aren't too many lasting associations in the entertainment field like the Patti Page—Jack Rael partnership." This was a great testament, indeed! "The only other such partnership I can recall was Kate Smith with Ted Collins," Jack continued. "I produced every record Patti made...except one, *Mockingbird Hill.*"

In 1947 Jack first hired Patti to sing with another one of his clients, the Jimmy Joy Band. With Jack's guidance she was featured in an important guest shot on a very popular, long-running radio show Don McNeill's *Breakfast Club*, one of radio's most listened to shows. Then Mercury records signed her up: "My first hit recording was *Confess* and my second was *With My Eyes Wide Open I'm Dreaming*," Patti recalled. "They were very exciting days for me." Jack had invented what he called "overdubs" where Patti would record the song several times over and then have it played back as if she were a group singing different harmonic parts, a practice later used by guitarist Les Paul and his wife Mary Ford.

Frankie Laine told me he was an early supporter of Patti Page. A Mercury Records A & R man asked him his professional opinion of Patti back in 1946 when she was first signed, and he and Carl Fischer, Frank's musical director, agreed she was terrific, "and bound for the big time, sooner or later," said Frankie.

"The first time I saw my name in lights," Patti said, "was when I played the Paramount Theater (in New York) with Frankie Laine. He's a wonderful man, and he'll always have a very special place in my heart."

Talking with Al Ham, from a *Music of Your Life* syndicated radio station in Los Angeles during the late eighties, Patti reminisced about her mega-hit *Tennessee Waltz*: "Well, that song was recorded mostly because of coincidence. Jack and I had an office in the Brill Building in New York and Jerry Wexler was at that time working for *Billboard* as one of their reviewers and critics.

"One Wednesday morning he met Jack in the Brill Building and said, 'Jack, we reviewed a record last night by Erskine Hawkins called the *Tennessee Waltz* and if Patti got a hold of it, I think it would be a smash.' That's how it first came across as a song.

"So, I had a record that was to be released before Christmas. We had a song called *Boogie Woogie Santa Claus,* which Mercury felt was *the* Christmas song of the year. They said: 'Put something that's nondescript on the other side. The rest is history. Today nobody ever heard of *Boogie Woogie Santa Claus,* but I sure am thankful that they've heard of *Tennessee Waltz.*" For the record, to coin a phrase, over seven million copies have been sold.

Patti grew up listening to her sister's record collection composed of Sinatra, Miller, Dorsey, and Shaw: "I didn't get to listen to the radio very much, but I did get to hear Dinah Shore when she was first on the Eddie Cantor Show...she was the greatest!"

Like Kay Starr and others, Patti never gets tired of singing her early hits, responsible, after all, for her success: "*Doggie in the Window* is not one of my favorites to sing, but musically I haven't gotten tired of singing *Cape Cod* and (Redd Stewart and Pee Wee King's) *Tennessee Waltz* because I have a lot of marvelous memories of all that happened to me during the time I recorded them, and the people love to hear them." As Kay Starr once enlightened me, during an interview,... "it gets the memories starting."

Patti told me the charming story about the origin of *Mockingbird Hill,* one of her best-known hits: "I was leaving Chicago, going to New York on my way to Miami to open at the Fountainbleu hotel, when I was paged at the airport. I went to the phone and it was Art Talmidge, a V.P. at Mercury Records.

"He said, 'Patti, don't take that plane. Wait out there for me. I'm coming out with a record that I want to play for you.' I canceled my flight. Art showed up with a little portable record player and played Les Paul and Mary Ford's rendition of *Mockingbird Hill.* He said, 'so I think we should cover it.'

"And I said, 'Well, okay. Jack is already in Florida and I've never recorded without him.' He told me not to worry about it and to get to New York, the recording date was all set up at Bob Fein's studio. I went there; we recorded just one side. He said, 'I promise you that I won't release it if Jack doesn't like it.' I left the next day for Miami and played it immediately for Jack. He called Art and said, 'I like the song; I think she did a good job on it, Art,' and Art said, 'Thank God, because we've already pressed 200,000 records and shipped them.' "

And, what do you know, Patti performed at Frank Palumbo's Click nightclub in Philadelphia in May of 1948 with none other than the Benny Goodman sextet, occasionally vocalizing on variations of *Limehouse Blues, Bye Bye Blues*, and *Indiana*, with the likes of jazz pianist Teddy Wilson and other notable bandleaders and top jazz-bop musicians of the time.

Patti worked for years, never missing an engagement except once. Being naturally shy in front of audiences, and working hard to keep her weight down, caused her to bomb at the New York Copacabana back in 1951. But, after the hits *I Went to Your Wedding, Doggie in the Window, Mockingbird Hill* (her theme and personal favorite), *This Is My Song* and ten years of experience and phenomenal recording success, she turned that all around, thank you, with a 1961 reappearance at the Copa to a rousing success.

155

Television beckoned in the early fifties when Patti was summoned to replace Perry Como on The Music Hall on NBC and then she starred on a filmed syndicated twice-a-week 15 minute, worldwide show that led to appearances on the *The Big Record* and eventually her very own, one-hour network show, *The Patti Page Show*, which lasted for three years. In 1991 she hosted a second reunion musical program for PBS (public television) with song stars the McGuire Sisters, Teresa Brewer, Maggie Whiting, Fran Warren, Julius LaRosa, and the New Ink Spots all appearing. The girls looked wonderful, not much different than when, as Teresa says, "you were putting another nickel in the jukebox." The show was taped at the Waldorf Astoria in New York.

The show *Jukebox Saturday Night* mirrored the way it was in those times. Patti's dress was stunning. She opened with Rodgers and Hart's *Where or When* and *When You're Smiling*, followed by Julie LaRosa singing his famous hits. Teresa Brewer bounced along with her perennial hit *Music Music, Music* and capped off with *Ricochet Romance*. My friend, the hip Fran Warren, moved the audience to tears with her never aging evergreen *Sunday Kind of Love*, and my absolute pal Margaret Whiting captured the audience with *Moonlight in Vermont,* her all time favorite. Patti wrapped up things with a medley of her all-time hits, too, as she wandered through the audience greeting them in a friendly way. The audience loved every moment. It's too bad these shows aren't presented more often on television, other than on pledge-week programs.

Patti Page appeared in the great motion picture *Elmer Gantry* that starred Burt Lancaster and Shirley Jones in Oscar winning performances. Patti played Gantry's mistress and chorus director. Patti also appeared with Kim Novak and James Garner in the film *Boys Night Out*.

Patti stills sings her way around the music world. Throughout the Eighties she toured from Boston to San Francisco, playing her first "gig" at the Fairmont Hotel which she had thought was a more jazz-oriented place. "I received a great reception from the audience. As I traveled around the country then, the response to my kind of music was greater than it had ever been."

156

The Song Stars of the Fifties enjoyed a new resurgence in the Eighties performing once again America's classic music that Tony Bennett once described to me as the timeless songs of Harold Arlen, Cole Porter, George Gershwin, Harry Warren, and Irving Berlin. That led to new interest in our Song Stars, their past recordings being re-issued on CD's by previously disinterested recording companies.

Patti Page, one of those Song Stars, is clearly one of the best-loved advertisements for America's popular music of the last 50 years. For a girl who never had singing lessons, never found it necessary to warm-up her voice before performances, and by 1965 had record sales of over 70 million, I'd say that's pretty good, wouldn't you? Jack Rael says, "She is the best singer there ever was." Then, Jack had to be the best manager there ever was to seal this remarkable partnership.

Thanks, Patti. Thanks, Jack.

The LENNON SISTERS

Jimmy Durante's "Goils"

The first question posed to the lovely Lennon Sisters, after four solid kisses planted one by one on their cheeks followed by a variety of giggles, was "Did Jimmy Durante really call you 'my goils?' " I asked them that one summer's night backstage at Westbury Music Fair.

"Oh! yes," replied Kathy. "He loved us and we loved him. We appeared with him on our joint television show in 1969."

I had just stepped into their dressing room after completing an interview with Nashville music legend Eddie Arnold. Eddie's manager, Jerry Purcell, unexpectedly invited us to meet the *other act* in the show, the precocious, grown-up Lennon Sisters—Janet, Kathy, Diane, and Peggy. Moments earlier Eddie Arnold was extolling their talents and raving about their backup performances on his show.

While I began the *inquisition*, my photographer Camille Smith did the camera clicking. "Where are you girls going these days....what's happening? It seems a long time since we've heard from you."

"Well...we travel...maybe four or five times a year —when it's beneficial money-wise for us to all go together." They all talked at once. "We have to support our stageman and drummer too. We usually back up people like Andy Williams and Eddy (Arnold) in places like Vegas and sometimes we travel as our own single act. We try to bring along some of the kids and husbands if we can...but at different times. We limit it to three or four trips a year....the most." The girls always sang those catchy, jaunty, specialty tunes they have been famous for.

"In what kinds of situations?"

"Places like this....theaters in the round...or at state fairs. We'll be moving on to Atlantic City right after this." *This* was 1986 and the four girls never looked lovelier or acted more enthusiastic, like kids on a carousel, each trying to grab the ring. The familiar faces with those infectious smiles made it an absolute joy to be with them.

"The youngest one is Janet, right?" They stood together with kimonos draped over their bodies, expecting to go onstage in about forty-five minutes. We had interrupted "make-up" time.

"That's me," answered Janet from behind. Janet was the most famous face of the Lennons.

"Is it true...at least that's what I have heard...that you quit (Lawrence) Welk because he would not give you a raise after a long time on a very low salary?" I presumptuously inquired to get things started.

"Basically, yes," answered Kathy, "We began with him—being four girls in one family...and he paid us scale. But we were there a long time at group scale and felt we deserved solo scale," they argued, "but, when we got married and were raising children and so on....what we took home...simply wasn't enough for the time we were spending away which was a full five days a week."

The girls had been with Welk for almost 12 years.

Welk had reasoned that they were gaining fame and attention appearing on his world-famous television show and that was to be considered a sort of payment. Welk was known to pay all his performers only scale. The girls took home only $100.00 each. He believed they could make fabulous sums at appearances at state fairs on their own time with the publicity they received from being on his show. The girls began in 1955 on Welk's Christmas Show and surprised the experts by drawing 30 million viewers almost every week.

"Oh, sure! It was a wonderful showcase for what it was, but we had gotten to the point where we needed to grow and so we ended up going on the road," said Kathy, who seemed to be general spokeswoman for the group.

"Leaving the Welk show came at a time when we wanted to grow musically and didn't want to be treated as little girls," piped up Janet, "and so this allowed us to leave town these four times a year and

159

make—FIFTY—times more money than to stay and do the Welk show. It worked out much better for us financially."

"Was Welk upset about it?" I asked. It was widely reported that he was.

"I don't know...we were with him for twelve-and-a half years. We loved him very much, and he us. He raised us. We were just little kids. There are no hard feelings. We had to make a change and maybe he didn't understand," they replied over camera directives and clicks.

The Lennons' sentimental ballads and sweet songs executed in close harmony was a welcome contrast for viewers and listeners compared to the rock and roll being promoted to the public at that time.

I reminded them that, when I would be watching the Welk show on television with my two daughters, the kids would refer to them as the "Lemmon Sisters" saying, "here come the Lemmons," all of this to great giggles and laughter from the girls. The Lennons were so gregarious and delightful.

"There are so many people we meet that played with our paper dolls and colored in our coloring books and now they're all the same age as we are and they are now parents like us. We grew up right alongside our fans, "Peggy was saying.

Camille dutifully posed the girls standing around a kneeling me, "This is going to be the best picture of my life," I said...to more giggles, "My daughters will kill for this."

Then, "O.K., girls. For the record I would like each one to state their name and age and how many children you have."

"All right...I'll start......I'm Peggy, and I'm married to Dick Cathheart and we have six children." Dick was a trumpet player in the Welk organization and was currently freelancing. "Married nineteen years next week."

"I'm Diane and married to Dick Gass and have three children, two girls eighteen and nineteen and a boy seventeen who plays in a rock band."

"Dick is a telephone repair man," I reported.

"How did you know?"

"Research, my dear young lady, research, "to even more infectious giggling.

"Okay! I'm Janet and married to John Bahler—second marriage—(the first to ABC page Lee Bernhardi and had three children) and have five children and am raising them all."

"Oh, God!" I muttered, "little Janet, an American institution is *married* with teenage children."

The girls infectious laughter brightened the room.

"I'm last...I'll finish off. I'm Kathy and married to Jim Derhris who is a chiropractor and we have no children and we've just been married one year. This is my second marriage. (The first was to Mahlon Clark, another Welk musician who also played with Ray McKinley's band.)

Back in those days the top programs were the *Ed Sullivan Show* on Sunday and *Lawrence Welk's* on Saturday nights. That was it for musical variety shows. Everybody knew where to find the Lennons.

"Now, when you go home and the show is over and all the lights are gone, what do you do?"

"We do what every other housewife does. We scrub floors and take care of our children and husbands," agreed Kathy. "We all live in L.A. and see each other almost every day. One of us teaches school." At the time there was not one pool or grandiose house among the four, even though they really could have afforded it.

"We spend our evenings watching television and enjoying our families," boasted Janet.

"We love our homes and family, and we also love our careers." said Diane," and all of our sons play in rock bands and perform at school."

"Do you all get along as sisters?" I treaded carefully with that one.

"Yes," said Diane, "We really do! We have seven other brothers and sisters, so we have a large family."

"When you are preparing for a tour, how do you get it all together?"

"When we put in new material, we learn the music, we learn the dancing. We rehearse and rehearse, but only the new stuff, otherwise we know our regular parts and need minimum rehearsing. Once it's up 'here,' " Janet said pointing to the brain behind her forehead, "we never have to rehearse it again."

161

The girls' appearance was a happy, upbeat, uptempo show with lots of close harmony. "We get to do old songs, new songs, production numbers with four costume changes, and thoroughly enjoyable vignettes."

"The audiences are incredible," the girls declared almost in unison, forever talking over one another, "there are always standing ovations every night."

"It's always a good, warm crowd," Janet Lennon reassured me.

Watching the show after the interview revealed an opening film clip projected on a large screen portraying their very first appearance on the Lawrence Welk show. The camera caught the girls constantly glancing to their left where their father was crouched in the wings— sort of directing them from offstage. It was amusing to see again, especially at this time with the girls now matured performers. The show was simply great as they had promised it would be. Their fans were vocal to say the least and, after the last performance, they rose to their feet and cheered.

The Lennons enjoyed that, and so did we.

Today the Lennons are singing with the Lawrence Welk Big Band in Branson, Missouri,...."everyday, for the rest of our lives," say the girls in one joint phrase.

A young Lynn Roberts poses with Jimmy Dorsey's boy singer Bob Eberly at the State Theater, Hartford, CT. (Lynn Roberts Collection)

**Tommy Dorsey "clips" Lynn Roberts ponytail in Las Vegas in 1954.
(Lynn Roberts Collection)**

LYNN ROBERTS

The Last of the Big Band Singers

I consider lovely Lynn Roberts to be the last and one of the best of the Big Band Era vocalists.

"I believe I was the only lady band singer who sang with both Tommy and Jimmy Dorsey, Harry James, and Benny Goodman—and not for just short periods," Lynn said. She and I were reminiscing about her association with those remarkable Big Bands. While other vocalists were well out on their own, Lynn, young and enthusiastic, was headlining the last years of those famous touring bands.

Born in Brooklyn, New York, but raised in Elmhurst, Queens, Leonore Theresa Raisig, like many other Song Stars, got off to an early start on the Horn and Hardart Children's Hour radio show in New York. "Then, before long I was appearing on Ted Steele's local afternoon television variety show. Irene Day, who was band leader Charlie Spivak's wife and former band singer for both Spivak and Gene Krupa, called me at the station after seeing the show and invited me to an audition along with many other hopefuls: 'My husband is looking for a female singer for our band. Would you be interested? ' she asked, and I responded with a definite —Yes! 'Then go to Nola Studios later today,' she advised.

"So I did and later that night they called with good news. I got the job for sixty dollars a week which was a lot of money then—I paid my own hotel bills and even sent money home to my mother. I was just 15 years old and I stayed on for one-and-a-half years."

"But like other singers Rosey Clooney and Doris Day, weren't you sort of young to tour from state to state with a group of men musicians on a bus?"

"Oh, sure! That's why my mother kept looking for a stay-in-New York kind of job for me. She discovered that Vincent Lopez, who was a steady attraction at the Taft Hotel in New York City, advertised for

165

A very young Lynn Roberts auditions.
(Lynn Roberts Collection)

a band singer. Mom got me an audition and I got the job. Then, while I was there, (Tommy) Dorsey's road manager spotted me one night while he was having dinner at the Taft and called me over and asked me to go with Dorsey."

"And.......?"

"What? Are you kidding? I couldn't wait. I went traveling on a bus again."

"I remember a short film that I have on video tape in which you were performing with both Jimmy and Tommy Dorsey in 1955 and your trademark ponytail was flying all over the place while you vocalized on one of the Dorsey's biggest hits *Yes. Indeed*! Wasn't there an anecdote about that infamous ponytail?" In the film Lynn was swinging her hips, snapping her fingers, almost unable to contain herself, her bright blonde hair bouncing back-and-forth from shoulder to shoulder in an infectious rhythm, her head swaying from side to side.

"Yup! Tommy fired me after five years because I wouldn't cut it off. He said he didn't like it anymore. So we had a big fight."

"What did you do?"

"I left the band.....for eight months. But while I was singing in a club in Montreal, Tommy came in to see me one night. He was sitting at the bar, so after my song I went over to say hello. He promptly asked me to come back because he was going to appear at the Paramount with Frank Sinatra. So I said OK."

"Did you have to cut off the ponytail as part of the deal?"

"No, I didn't!" she said triumphantly to my expected grin.

Lynn considers the high point of her career to be that very performance at the New York Paramount Theater with Frank Sinatra and Tommy Dorsey in 1956. "It was the end of a great era," Lynn fondly reminisced, "shortly after Tommy and Jimmy were both gone."

"By the way," she said, "That video you have was from a movie short filmed in 1954 and it was called *The Dorsey Brothers Encore*. Actually I had been with Tommy when Jimmy joined up with him in 1953. It was known as the "Last Fabulous Dorsey Brothers Band." As you know, Tommy died suddenly in 1956. He had a big meal and was in the throes of a terrible divorce and had taken some sleeping pills...he became sick and couldn't wake up...it was a nightmare. He was only 51 years old. Everyone was in shock."

"Yes, I remember that day. The entire music world was stunned. I recall Warren Covington telling me the story," I recalled to Lynn, "he said it was the band's day off from a lengthy "gig" at the Statler Hotel's Cafe Rouge' in New York."

I asked Lynn about her duration with Harry James.

167

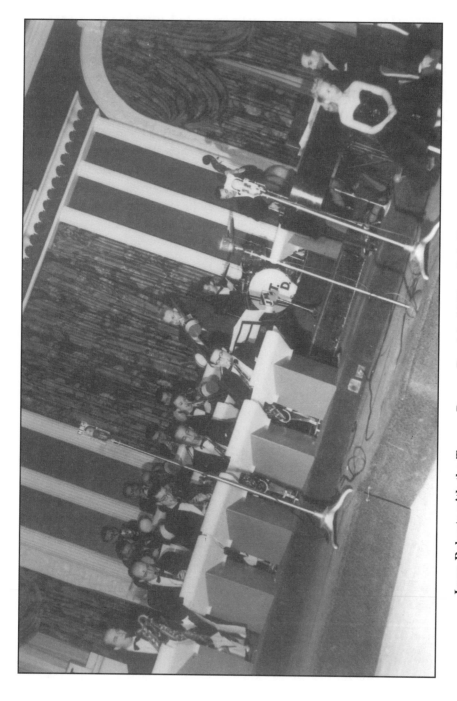

Lynn Roberts with the Tommy Dorsey Band in 1953 at Cafe Rouge, New York City.
(Lynn Roberts Collection)

"Let's see! I started in 1978 and remained with him until he passed away in 1983." Harry had considered Lynn to be one of his best vocalists ever, according to Harry James expert Joe Pardee of the Harry James Appreciation Society. Joe was kind enough to present me with a personally narrated five tape gift highlighting Harry, his band personnel and his vocalists. Some of those recordings prove Lynn's worthiness as an impressive Big Band vocalist.

"I remember watching you rehearse when I interviewed Harry in '82, but you were busy with the band out front and I had to get to Westbury Music Fair for another interview and was running late," I explained.

Lynn considers her personal best recording to be all her recordings, although she confesses to being over-critical of her work. "But, I think probably my favorite is the tribute album I did for Harry James." The MGM album, *Harry, You Made Me Love You,* was released in 1983, just after Harry's passing.

"But, between Tommy and Harry, wasn't there a time you worked with the Pied Pipers?"

"Oh, sure! In the Seventies Warren Covington owned and managed the Pipers and I was the lead singer for about five years. Sometimes Warren would sing the 'Sinatra' stuff, backed by the group like they did in the '40's with Tommy. I liked the way Warren sang and managed things. It was a great experience for me."

Lynn has her personal favorites, too! Keely Smith is one of the singers she likes today, but her all-time favorite female vocalist is Jo Stafford. (Just a few days ago, while talking to Jo Stafford, I recounted what Lynn said about her. Jo was both appreciative and gratified.)

As for male vocalists: "I love Torme' and I love Tony Bennett, but Sinatra—well, there will never be anyone like him ever again."

Lynn worked with Benny Goodman for ten years beginning in 1961. She sang with the band and toured Europe with the sextet too and is featured on the *Benny Goodman Reader's Digest Album.* On the sensitive subject of relationships with legendary Benny Goodman, many vocalists have complained about his riveting "Goodman Ray," where he would stare menacingly at players and singers when he disapproved of one thing or another. "I thought I knew how to handle Benny, and I did for a long while. But one day I got the 'ray,'" she said, "I won't tell you why, but I will tell you I have probably the only letter of apology Benny ever wrote and it hangs prominently on my wall." There was also the amusing story about how Lynn once complained to Benny that it was cold in the studio: "So Benny left the studio and came back wearing a sweater," she laughed about it.

As now a long time one-girl act, Lynn has appeared at Michael's Pub in New York, toured Israel with the Mel Lewis orchestra, and was featured at Osaka Symphony Hall in Japan in their very first jazz concert ever. The year 1993 found her as the highlight of a Palm Beach, Florida, tribute to Carnegie Hall. "Gigs" at Tavern on the Green and The Rainbow Room and other jazz venues have been regular events for her over the years.

The Palm Beach concert reviews encapsulated my own personal feelings about Lynn Roberts: One newspaper said, "...on stage she had no affectations and appeared to love what she was doing. Her voice shows no sign of age; it was crystal clear and beautifully controlled. Her charm and enthusiasm coupled with a great vocal style made her the absolute hit of the show." Lynn has always been the hit of the show. Even New York critic Rex Reed, compliment miser, says, "......Lynn sings like an angel."

If you want to hear Lynn Roberts at her best, get her newest CD album, *Lynn Roberts—The Men in My Life*—devoted to songs made popular by both Harry James and the Dorseys, as well as some of the others.

Just today Lynn sent me some wonderful photos including one rare snapshot with Tommy Dorsey pretending to "clip" her infamous ponytail on a day off alongside a swimming pool in Las Vegas. I gave her a call to tell her the priceless photos arrived in good condition. She had just returned from a Doc Severinsen big band hit parade concert with the Buffalo Philharmonic Pops on January 10. "The *Buffalo News* said the show was terrific. We got great reviews. Bobby Haggart (trumpet player) was in the show. Doc did the *Woodchopper's Ball*. It was a sold-out performance. I sang *Green Eyes, Tangerine, Sentimental Journey,* and *It's Been a Long, Long, Time*. I love singing those wonderful, enduring songs," she said, "I had a great time."

Lynn Roberts' lifetime of achievement with the biggest of the Big Bands and beyond clearly certifies her rightful place in music history among all the other great Song Stars who appear between the covers of this book.

170

Lynn Roberts brand-new photo January 1997.
(Courtesy Lynn Roberts)

Diana Krall sings; Benny Carter plays pure jazz.
(Photo Jazztree)

DIANA KRALL

Jazz's Vocal Future Is Bound for Glory

The good news is spreading. There is a young, smart, and lovely jazz pianist-vocalist on the scene who plays a superlative piano and sings like a fine instrument. She's new; she's good.

If you surf the internet music forums, you inevitably wander into the music message areas where you will find exchange boards on jazz trumpeters, pianists, vocalists, sax players, and drummers. Here you merge into ongoing arguments about who is the best among them, past or present. On-liners file news items, opinions and experiences with or about those *selected* performers. Participants from all over the world help one another locate whereabouts of their favorite artists' past or present recordings or the locations of latest and future appearances and file comments about past performances. The name Diana Krall appears regularly in those forums alongside more well-known, established performers. Internet subscribers rate her up there with Abbey Lincoln, Betty Carter, Shirley Horn, Cassandra Wilson, and Dinah Washington. Participants keep urging their peers to check out this young, breezy, upcoming, wispy voiced pianist-Song Star. Some comments were: "She sounds a lot like Carmen McRae," or "She's another Ella—reborn."

In a recent moment during dinner at Sophie's Restaurant in Smithtown, New York, a handful of patrons were trying to distinguish Diana while the host secretly played her latest album over the restaurant's sound system *Diana Krall—All for You, a Dedication to the Nat King Cole Trio* was sent to me by The Jazz Tree, Diana's management agency in New York. I asked restaurant manager Greg Armine to play it for us as sort of a "blindfold test" like those Leonard Feather used to hold in his regular *Downbeat Magazine* feature.

John the bartender opined: "...sounds a little like Sarah Vaughan.....who is she?" Sophie's son Chef Angelo at one point swore it must have been Peggy Lee, and Greg Armine insisted Diana sounded much like singer-pianist Shirley Horn. Sophie thought Diana reminded her of a mature Ella Fitzgerald. A patron thought it was Julie London.

They were all sort of right. Diana doesn't belt out a song but will take some chances in phrasing, expressing her repertoire coolly. Her piano swings graciously. Then, a casual glance at Diana's album photo also surprised everyone. She is extremely pretty. She is very young, just thirty. Her long blonde tresses suggest a glamorous movie star, not a jazz singer. "Wow!" they said unanimously, "she's really beautiful, too." Some critics have tagged her as a Sharon Stone look-alike.

Interesting to note that Dick LaPalm, once Nat Cole's publicist, wrote to Diana extolling her work on the album because it emulated his "ol'pal, Nathaniel, and you did it with perfect aplomb. My heartfelt thanks, Diana," he wrote, ".....I want to tell the whole world about you."

Diana's family was always involved in the love of music in one way or another. Her uncle sang a lot like Bing Crosby, and her father played stride piano, emulating the strains of the great Fats Waller. "We sang all kinds of stuff, old pop tunes, Fats Waller songs—everything. My grandmother's favorite was *Hard Hearted Hannah*," Diana proudly said, "and Dad has every recording Fats Waller ever made. He has an incredible collection of music, including the old cylinders—so I heard of lot of music from the time when recording began." She admits being influenced by Claude Thornhill, the bandleader who recorded *Sunday Kind of Love* with my friend, Song Star Fran Warren, and Jean Goldkette, prolific bandleader of the Thirties whose band members included Glenn Miller; Joe Venuti; my long time friend, pioneer arranger Bill Challis, a distinct Diana Krall influence; Charlie Spivak; and Artie Shaw.

Dave McKenna and, most importantly, Nat "King" Cole were later influences. Cole's trio instrument arrangement of piano, bass and guitar—minus drums—fascinated her. Diana is also seriously

Pretty, perky Diana Krall at her piano.
(Photo Jazztree)

interested in the works of Nina Simone, Shirley Horn, and Roberta Flack.

So, this young, vivacious lady piano player and jazz vocalist left her Nanaimo, British Columbia, home to seek her fortune in the world of jazz. After having studied classical piano since the age of four, performing with the high school jazz band, and actually performing three nights a week at a local restaurant, she felt ready for further training and, with a music scholarship in her pocket, signed up with Boston's Berklee College of Music (the largest private music college in the U.S., whose patron saint is Duke Ellington). She stayed on for 18 months studying piano with emphasis on jazz in the style of Nat "King" Cole. So her association with the Big Bands of the past was very much alive in her heart. With the strong influences of those Big Bands imbued in her character, musical views and training, Diana Krall was now getting ready to take on the world.

Back home she met drummer Jeff Hamilton and bassist John Clayton, opening the floodgates of opportunity. The meetings led to further study with pianist Jimmy Rowles, a veteran of Benny Goodman; Tommy Dorsey; and Bob Crosby, in California. She also learned a lot of bass lines from elegant pianist Dave McKenna, long associated with trumpeter Bobby Hackett. "I have always loved Dave since high school and I've got all his records."

Back in Toronto, she finished her training with multi-instrumentalist Don Thompson, formerly active in L.A. with the likes of Charlie Parker and Boyd Raeburn's Orchestra. "Don gave me lessons while I was in high school and it was great to be back with him," she said. During this period Diana polished her singing skills as well.

The early Nineties found Diana performing in Europe with Ray Brown on a "gig" in Geneva, Switzerland; for a week in Paris; and in the 1995 North Sea Festival in Holland. Bassist Ray Brown admittedly is her "godfather." The great veteran of Oscar Peterson's group is her personal friend. Diana certainly hangs out in excellent company with the cream of jazz.

In August of 1996, Diana appeared in her New York cabaret debut in the 90 seat Oak Room at New York's Algonquin Hotel, a famous venue for current music greats. It led the Wall Street Journal to declare "Diana Krall is bound for glory."

Once when Diana was appearing at a small hotel lounge, customers would ask, "Where's the piano player?" She'd reply, "I *am* the piano player."

Her recent appearance in Carnegie Hall in a tribute to saxophonist Benny Carter was a personal smash. She sang Carter's classic tune *Fresh Out of Love.*

Diana revels in the rich tradition that is jazz: "My idea of a fun evening," she says, "is to sit around with my records of Billie Holiday, Ella Fitzgerald, Sarah Vaughan, and pianists like Bill Evans and Art Tatum, and put them on the turntable one after another." Diana's passion for the old music reminds me of young singer Tom Postilio, whose chapter appears in the first book in this series, *The Best Damn Trumpet Player.* His experiences parallel those of Diana Krall in that they both learned America's classic music, a phrase coined by Tony Bennett, very early in their life.

Call me in a few years and remind me of my intuitive prediction that Diana Krall will indeed take her place among the finest Song Stars who ever graced a bandstand or faced a microphone. Just watch-n-see!

Connie Boswell 1939.
(Richard Grudens Collection)

MORE LADIES WHO SANG WITH THE BANDS

Ivie Anderson, Duke Ellington's classic performer on the original 1932 recording *It Don't Mean a Thing if It Ain't Got That Swing* and *Mood Indigo*, died too young and is still missed. Ivie was the Duke's best fitting to-the-orchestra-style singer. When she sang *Stormy Weather* at the London Palladium, some of the audience broke down and cried. Favorite Ellington recordings with Ivie include *When My Sugar Walks Down the Street* and a silly song, *Love Is Like a Cigarette*. She joined Ellington's band at just the right time, 1931, at the peak of his career, and became the band's first regular singer.

Ivie Anderson learned her craft while living in a convent. The vaudeville circuit was her venue for many years and included the Cotton Clubs in New York and L.A. She had the distinction of being the first black vocalist to sing with a white band. The band was the Anson Weeks Orchestra, a two-beat style band, featured for years at the Mark Hopkins Hotel in San Francisco. Ivie was just the right vocalist, interpreting the Duke's sensitive tunes. Everyone agrees— critics and musicans alike—that, although Ellington had a succession of female vocalists during the ensuing years, Ivie was the most sensitive and most talented of them all. "...Every girl singer we've had since Ivy had to prevail over her image," Duke Ellington said in his 1973 biography, *Music Is My Mistress,* "She was our good luck charm. We always broke performance records when Ivie was with the band." Ivie's sensitive singing was featured in the 1936 Marx Brothers film *A Day at the Races* for which the Duke composed some of the music.

Ivie left Duke Ellington in 1942 because of illness, but not before the great recording of *I Got It Bad and That Ain't Good* was waxed in 1941. She died at the age of forty-five from asthma. On a brighter note, Ivie Anderson was very successful with a Los Angeles restau-

179

Pearl Bailey 1955.
(Richard Grudens Collection)

rant called The Chicken Shack where she earned a comfortable living in her *off* years.

Pearl Bailey was born in Newport News, Virginia, in 1918 and her first band association was with the Cootie Williams Orchestra after she won a singing contest at the Apollo theater. She also sang with the bands of Noble Sissle, Edgar Hayes, and Cab Calloway in various nightclubs in Washington D.C., Baltimore, and New York. A definite jazz singer, but more a Broadway show singer, Pearl was especially acclaimed for her appearance in the all-black version of *Hello Dolly*. She married jazz drummer Louis Bellson and performed in many Las Vegas shows. Pearl sang in the movies *Porgy and Bess*, *Carmen Jones*, *That Certain Feeling* and *All the Fine Young Cannibals*. She had appeared many times with Bing Crosby on his various television shows. Her books, *The Raw Pearl* and *Talking to Myself*, classify her insights and experiences where, she says, "....I offered up my life's experiences for all to examine." We lost Pearl in 1990 after years of ill health.

Connee Boswell (lead singer of the Boswell Sisters), who shored up the bands of both Dorseys, Red Nichols, and Don Redman, too, was also the arranger for the singing Boswells. She was Bing Crosby's favorite female partner on the Kraft Music Hall and an early role model for Ella Fitzgerald on "scat" singing. A brave girl confined to a wheelchair most of her career due to an early bout with polio, Connee excelled on piano, sax and trombone too.

The three Boswell Sisters, Connee (earlier Connie), Martha, and Vet (for Helvetia), who sang earlier as a pre -Andrews Sisters group, were far ahead of their time. They arrived on the music scene in 1925, became nationally prominent in 1931 and were quickly acclaimed. Her family members were her mentors as they all sang together in quartets. The sisters could play many instruments and performed earlier as an instrumental group then graduated to vocalizing, after experimenting with their creative, special sounds. They worked so long and hard together developing their vocal capacity that they became always instantly in tune with one another. After her sisters left the act, Connee continued as a single, setting early styles of jazz-oriented "scat" singing. Her best recordings were *They Can't Take That Away from Me, The Loveliness of You, That Old Feeling, Bob White, The Waterfront,* and *Stormy Weather.* Connee passed away on October 12, 1976, at the age of 69. I'm thankful Patty Andrews and the Andrews Sisters came along and continued the great tradition of the excellent Boswells, aren't you?

Betty Carter, a stylist of extraordinary effort who goes strongly against the contemporary grain, has a cult following like Song Star Carmen McRae, but found it hard to appeal to larger audiences. In the 1970's she pulled everything together, closing out her Billie Holiday mode. Her individualistic representation of herself presents a calm but intense quality in her jazz phrasings. Betty was one of the really few singers who improvised with feeling. She drew her listeners into her songs. Backed by her own trio, she appeared in clubs, concerts and college dates in 1972. Some have nominated Betty Carter to "scat" knighthood, so to speak. She worked as hard at it as any sax player. People either love or hate Betty's style of jazz-scat-singing. Although some consider her the logical heir to Ella's work, Betty was strictly her own lady and represented jazz in the modern mode. Her *What a Little Moonlight Can Do* contains the best examples of her kind of "scatting."

Born Lillie Mae Jones in 1929, Betty honed her skills in church work. In 1947 she had the opportunity to sing with Charlie Parker's Quintet, her first contact with professionals. She joined up with Lionel Hampton: "I knew she was good, so I hired her as soon as I heard her sing at the audition," Hamp told me, "but we kinda had our problems." Betty went on to appear with jazz star Miles Davis and toured with Sonny Rollins in Japan. She recorded with Ray Charles in the late Fifties. Betty fell victim to the '60's rock era, but prevailed later with recordings like *Spring Can Really Hang You Up the Most,* performed with a trio, her best setting musically.

June Christy. Born in Springfield, Illinois, in 1925, June was the heir apparent to Anita O'Day who found June, whose real name was Shirley Luster, in 1945 performing at a Chicago nightclub called The Three Deuces. O'Day was weary of performing and traveling with the

Stan Kenton's June Christy 1955.
(Don Kennedy Collection)

Stan Kenton band and told June she would be leaving the band and advised her to audition for the job. June sounds a lot like O'Day. She was pretty, blond, bright, friendly and very well liked by her fellow performers. Her recordings of *Tampico* and *Willow Weep for Me* in 1945 were great commercial successes.

She began it all at age thirteen singing with a local band then joined the Boyd Raeburn band in Chicago. After recovering from scarlet fever, she sang with Benny Strong's band and performed at the Three Dueces. While with Kenton, June married (and stayed married) to tenor sax player Bob Cooper who was a member of the band. In 1954 she made an album entitled *Something Cool* her best work for my money. Critics say the song *Something Cool* itself is owned lock, stock and barrel by June Christy alone. Other attempts to vocalize it have failed miserably. My favorite Christy recording is Benny Carter's 1958 version of *When Lights Are Low*, arranged by her husband Bob. She is also accompanied by Bob playing with the Kenton band. It's typical cool, husky Christy.

June went into semi-retirement in the late '60's, after recording her last album at Capitol records, emerging occasionally for night club engagements in the Hollywood area. In 1972 she made a guest appearance with Kenton at the Newport Jazz Festival. Chris Connor followed June into the Kenton Band. The three girls' singing styles and sounds were very much alike, although Anita was the original, the peppiest, and the most innovative. Nevertheless, June Christy is a wonderful Song Star and deserves recognition here. She has always been a Big Band singer and felt uncomfortable in small combos. Stanton bassist Eddie Safranski, an old friend of mine from NBC studio days, once told me he preferred the voice of June Christy over any band singer he has known or worked with. A worthy tribute from a worthy musician.

Blossom Dearie, a Song Star with meritorious cocktail piano and song-writing skills, draws out all the expressive qualities of a song. She worked with Woody Herman, and her efforts with The Blue Stars vocal group in Paris were simply first-rate. I love the recording *It Amazes Me* (written by my old NBC lunch time, piano-playing pal Cy Coleman and lyricist Carolyn Leigh), recorded in 1959 and backed with Mundel Lowe's experienced guitar, Ray Brown's bass, and her own piano and vocalizing. Blossom is elegant, polite, and funny, too! She lights up the songs she sings. The little girl, squeaky quality denotes her singing personality. A composer, too, she wrote her hits *I Like You, You're Nice* and *Hey John*. Blossom Dearie was first a pianist, sitting in with the likes of The Modern Jazz Quartet and others. Doubling on voice was a second career that came a little later. Blossom commands her own special audiences with a faithful following. Her singing has always been simply pleasant with an *unvaried* repertoire you could count on.

Ruth Etting, the happy singer of sad songs, was once called The Sweetheart of Columbia Records. Her renditions of *Ten Cents a Dance* (her most famous delineation and my own favorite), *Shaking The Blues Away*, and *It All Depends on You* always made me realize what an excellent song interpreter she could be. Born in David City, Nebraska, in 1905, she was a very accomplished white blues singer, sometimes described as a "torch singer," and very adept and glamorous. She could have been a jazz singer, as her grasp of the idiom, her tasteful phrasing and occasional improvising lifted many a poor song from mediocrity and charmingly counter-pointed the recording sessions with jazz as a base. The film *Love Me or Leave Me* was a Doris Day, Jimmy Cagney Hollywood account of Ruth's 1920's career, the title being one of her best known recordings. Ruth Etting's association with the Big Bands was limited to her work with Art Kahn's Dance Band, Paul Whiteman's King of Jazz Orchestra, the *first* Big Band, and with Abe Lyman's society style orchestra in Chicago. She was often backed by jazz artists guitarist Eddie Lang, jazz violinist Joe Venuti, and Tommy and Jimmy Dorsey. She retired to a delightful little ranch in Colorado, where she said, and sang *"It All Belongs to Me."*

Helen Humes sang with Harry James and Benny Goodman. Her best number was *Between the Devil and the Deep Blue Sea* with Basie in 1939. While with Count Basie's band in 1938, Jimmy Rushing was the blues singer, so she was usually assigned ballads too. The expressive shading in her delivery was usually thrown away when she sang the blues. Count Basie first discovered Helen Humes at the Cincinnati Cotton Club in 1937. She cut many sides with Basie including *Thursday*, *Blame It on My Last Affair* and *Sing for Your Supper*.

She quit the harsh life of road tours in 1941 and began her club appearances in New York City. She later settled in California then joined up with impresario Norman Granz for the *Jazz at the Philharmonic* series. In the '50's Helen recorded with many companies and contributed to movie sound tracks. It was with Basie again in a television film entitled *Showtime at the Apollo*, followed by tours to Australia with Red Norvo in the Sixties. *Downbeat* once rated her with Ella Fitzgerald and Mildred Bailey as one of the best singers of the Big Band Era.

Helen "retired" in 1967 taking work in a munitions factory in Louisville, Kentucky, because she felt agents were no longer interested in her. She emerged in 1973 when friends convinced her to revise her singing life. During her autumnal revival of the 1970's, she shifted from blues singer to ballad singer, proving her merit. Her personal favorite, *Every Now and Then,* which she recorded in February 1975, accompanied by pianist Ellis Larkins and Buddy Tate's tenor sax, underlined her ability as a balladeer. Some say she sounded better at the age of sixty than when she was in her prime. She was still swinging in 1980, the year before her death, with tenor sax player Buddy Tate and his band.

Abbey Lincoln. I had the pleasure of talking to Abbey and Mel Torme' at the Oyster Bay, Long Island, jazzfest last season and she (and he) are still perfection in jazz. It was my son Bill's introduction to jazz singing. Bill is a devoted fan of Genesis star Phil Collins. Abbey Lincoln (real name, Anna Marie Woolridge) altered his musical perpective forever. Her most prominent work was sans the Big Bands, but work with composer Max Roach, to whom she was once married, was excellent and established her as a formidable jazz/blues singer. Her over 35 year career has been a steady progression of changes in singing style. Known earlier as Gaby Lee, Abbey was a supper-club favorite dishing up Billie Holiday stuff. Under the pseudonym Aminata Moseka, she wrote her own songs, including the lyrics for Thelonious Monk's *Blue Monk*, which she recorded in 1961 backed by Coleman Hawkins' legendary tenor sax. Abbey Lincoln is still growing while performing. Her clear African-influenced repertoire is unconventional jazz, but that night in Oyster Bay she proved her worth as her sobriquet, The First Lady of Modern Jazz. She reminds me of Billie Holiday more than any of the modern jazz singers. The talk-sing phrasing does it.

Carmen McRae. A clipped, precise delivery, even more pronounced than Dinah Washington's, is Carmen McRae's trademark. There is no doubt of the respect she commanded in the jazz community. A piano playing vocalist, Carmen appeared with the bands of Benny Carter and Mercer Ellington during the 1940's.

She was saw the light of day in Harlem, New York, and took formal piano lessons before winning a talent contest at the famed Apollo Theater. There she met Billie Holiday, whom she described as her hero, and who she said instilled encouragment into her and advised her to persevere if she wanted to be successful as a singer. A solo vocalist since then, Carmen continued to tour, especially in Japan during the 1960's and '70's. She sang with Benny Carter's big band in 1944 and went on to perform with Count Basie and Earl Hines. She completed more than 20 albums including *I Am Music* and *You Can't Hide Love*, my favorites. She played the clubs in L.A. and vicinity and made many recordings, including a great version of *Some Other Spring* in 1961. She is a veteran of many jazz festivals and is revered by a legion of fans, even now. In a recording done in Japan entitled *Carmen Alone,* she sang and played piano, illustrating her excellent repertoire. In the 1980's she performed on an RCA album *Carmen Sings Monk..* It was a great attempt to vocalize Monk's quirky melodies.

An asthma sufferer, she sometimes performed while sitting on a stool and was bedridden at the end of her life. Her last public performance was in 1991 at one of her favorite singing residences, New York's Blue Note club, where she became ill.

Carmen, one of the Big Band Era's premier vocalists and a distinct favorite among jazz musicians, died in Beverly Hills on November 10, 1994.

Dinah Shore swings with Count Basie 1941. (Jack Ellsworth Collection)

"Her sometimes gruff, smoky voice was allied with an acute feeling for rhythm and harmony and a bitter-sweet sense of humour." said *The London Times* in November of 1994.

Carmen McRae was considered part of the troika of female American jazz singers that included both Ella and Sarah.

Dinah Shore. When Fanny Rose Shore came to New York, she landed a non-paying job at New York radio station WNEW. The program manager, sensing her talent, arranged an audition with Martin Block, legendary disc jockey of *Make Believe Ballroom* fame, and she sang the song *Dinah*. Block accidentally introduced her on the air as Dinah Shore, forgetting her first name. "I was so grateful," Dinah said later in an interview, "that I never corrected him." She sang on WNEW with another unknown youngster, Frank Sinatra. She became popular in the late 1930's, when she could be heard singing with the *Chamber Music Society of Lower Basin Street* and on the *Eddie Cantor Show* as a "regular." Dinah was one of Cantor's many successful proteges. She also once sang with the Leo Reisman Orchestra in 1939 and the enthusiastic Peter Dean "scat"-singing band around the same period.

Some of Dinah's best were: *Yes, My Darling Daughter, Dear Hearts and Gentle People,* and *Buttons and Bows* from the Bob Hope film *Paleface*. Dinah was not entirely a product of the Big Bands; she prevailed during the period from roughly 1947 to 1953, although she was once almost hired by Woody Herman-almost. Was he sorry later! Later, she was a featured star on her own long-running TV show where she would always close the show throwing a kiss at the camera with a memorable, lovable grunt...*mm.m.m.m.m.muh!*

Keely Smith. Mostly identified as the singer who made it with her then husband, trumpet player and bandleader Louis Prima, on the 1958 blockbuster recording of *Old Black Magic*, Song Star Keely Smith is still actively singing today. Frances Langford just told me she loves to listen to Keely, saying: "She has such a great singing voice—I love to listen to her." Fellow singers Dolly Dawn and Frankie Laine also expressed their admiration of Keely Smith. Louis and Keely played a lot of Las Vegas "gigs" in the '60's where they had a strong following. Keely Smith works very hard today for down-and-out singers as a member of the Advisory Council of the Society of Singers in L.A.

Maxine Sullivan was the Song Star vocalist known as the *Loch Lomand* girl after her 1937 noteworthy, Claude Thornhill recording of that song. The wonderful bell-like quality sound in her voice mixed with remarkable musical integrity is Maxine's trademark. Her 1937 version of Irving Berlin's *Blue Skies*—not exactly a folk song— brought a different feeling to jazz singing. Maxine played valve trombone and trumpet, too. In the Sixties, Maxine actually worked as a nurse, busy with community affairs in the Bronx, New York. In her 1967 comeback at a New York Town Hall, she prevailed. Next, Maxine toured with the World's Greatest Jazzband from 1969 through 1975, including an appearance at the Newport, Rhode Island, Jazz Festival. Even at the age of 64, Maxine was still singing with that gentle swinging quality that established her originally.

"Liltin" **Martha Tilton** followed Helen Ward in the Benny Goodman band. She appeared in the famous 1938 Carnegie Hall Concert, showing up in an expensive pink tulle dress she bought at Lord & Taylor for the occasion. There she sang *Loch Lomand*, a swing rendition of a Scottish song recorded previously by Maxine Sullivan that past summer. Martha previously sang with Jimmy Dorsey. She projected a wholesome girl-next-door appearance and was very attractive. She stayed with Benny for two years. In 1939 she dominated all Benny Goodman recordings for RCA Victor with great numbers like *And the Angels Sing* (which she sang once again in 1994 at a Society of Singers party in LA) and *Bei Mir Bist du Schoen* (accompanied by Ziggy Elman's great trumpet), among others. She appeared in the 1956 movie *The Benny Goodman Story,* personally selected by Benny himself, along with other veterans of the band, for the sound track.

Bea Wain is the Song Star whose wonderful rendition of two great songs, *Deep Purple* and *My Reverie*, recorded with Larry Clinton's Orchestra, will live forever. Together with her husband, radio announcer supreme Andre' Baruch, they were known as Mr. & Mrs

Music on New York's WMCA. Andre' was the original announcer on the *Kate Smith* and the *Fred Waring Shows* and Bea was in the chorus in both. "That's how we started together," said Bea, "That's how it happened. We began dating."

Bea started with the Kay Thompson singing group. "We were 13 girls and 3 boys. Most of the kids in the chorus did not read notes. We would learn songs by listening to Kay on the piano. She would play a chord. The low voices would watch her thumb. The middle voices would watch her middle finger. And the high voices would watch her pinkie. When she played we followed her fingers and we got a great spontaneous sound. I was very proud to be in that group."

Bea Wain represented a certain class with a very distinctive sound. On all her recordings Bea is easily identified as a *bona fide* New Yorker. When she vocalizes *You Go to My Head* or *My Heart Belongs to Daddy*, you can grasp the feeling. I love her impeccable voice. I always imagined Bea Wain singing all her famous songs in a lavishly furnished, royally appointed living room somewhere in the Waldorf Astoria Hotel. Bea graduated to the Larry Clinton Band, whose own fame leans a lot on this terrific Song Star. In the late Thirties she sang on radio's *Hit Parade* with husband Andre' doing the announcing chores. Read the footnote on the Ella Fitzgerald segment of this book for a charming insight into the life of Ella as told by her friend Bea Wain. Bea's efforts today consist of special performances and her great work as Secretary with the Society of Singers. I and others wonder what would have happened if Bea had stayed and recorded with other bands besides Clinton's?

Helen Ward got her jump-start with the Benny Goodman Band just as the band took off during the ground-breaking 1934 Palomar Ballroom swing-fest. Helen was a New York girl singing with a New York voice and later broke her own ground with Eddy Duchin's and Will Osborne's Orchestras. My friend Willard Alexander, who represented Benny, helped hitch Helen to the high-flying Goodman Band. He knew her swinging rhythms worked well with Benny's new style. However, Helen never remained with one band, preferring the *independent* road. She was subsequently featured with the bands of Teddy Wilson, Harry James, Gene Krupa, and even Hal McIntyre, but never

Benny Goodman's Helen Ward 1936.
(Jack Ellsworth Collection)

stayed very long with any of them. Some consider her the archetypical band singer, widely imitated, closely followed by those who followed her. She was quick and snappy and employed an exuberance that was contagious.

After some work in radio as a producer, Helen Ward joined with a Goodman comeback in the early '50's and performed again with Larry Clinton on some album work. Her 1953 rendition of *What a Little Moonlight Can Do* is my personal Helen Ward favorite.

Dinah Washington and Lionel Hampton go back a long way too. Here's the way the exuberant "Hamp" told it to me: "A little girl named Ruth Lee Jones, who worked in the powder room of Garrett's Bar in Chicago where I was playing and sometimes worked for Walter Fuller's Quintet, came out and sang for me. I liked her and I hired her on the spot. I instantly changed her name to Dinah Washington, but she didn't care what I called her so long as I gave her a job with my band. I don't know how I came up with that name, but she took it and became famous with it."

"Hamp" had a good eye for talent, having also discovered jazz singer Joe Williams on the very same day. Dinah stayed with the band for about a year. Before that, she toured with the Sallie Martin Gospel Singers. Her gutsy style, unique phrasing, and feeling for the blues transcended category. Among the blues ladies during the interim of Bessie Smith to Aretha Franklin, Dinah Washington emerged fitfully from the world of rhythm-and-blues to successfully embrace a popular repertoire.

She began, as so many others have, as a gospel singer and offered a taste of what a trained gospel singer could do when shifting gears into jazz blues and more popular music. Her recording with Hampton, *Salty Papa Blues,* is a blues classic; *Baby, Get Lost* and *Bitter Earth* were two of her best early hits. Her remarkably powerful mezzo-soprano voice was driven with sharp attacks and a fiery, swinging drive. On her recording of *That Ole Devil* you can hear distinct influences of Billie Holiday. Quincy Jones rates his album made with Dinah Washington, *Swingin' Miss D,* as one of the best albums he ever made. "Dinah Washington was fantastic, the greatest person I've ever worked for," said Fred Norman, Tommy Dorsey and Char-

Dinah Washington.
(Richard Grudens Collection)

lie Spivak trombonist and arranger, "She amazed me at one of our first sessions by recording a number in one take. 'That's it!' she said 'I know,' said I. "

A lot of people thought Dinah Washington was sort of a rough character, but it wasn't true. Once when she had a record date in Detroit where she also owned a restaurant, she would spend weeks supervising and handling the cash at the restaurant, not thinking about music at all. When one of the musicians finally got up the nerve to approach and ask her about working out of the sounds required for an upcoming date, she replied: "Oh, don't worry about that, sonny. You go back to New York, and I'll pick the tunes." She dutifully went back to the cash register.

A string of hits on the Mercury labels were: *What a Difference a Day Makes, It Could Happen to You, Our Love Is Here to Stay,* and *For All We Know*. These are the gems for which Dinah is more remembered. You can still hear them playing somewhere everyday.

She made a good song mean something. The terse, sardonic quality, the personal meaning she gave to every lyric, and the gutty timbre are all strikingly in evidence with every performance. My favorite recordings, consummated in 1961, were *Unforgettable* and *September in the Rain*. Dinah made many albums including *The Bessie Smith Songbook*, a tribute to someone she both admired and emulated. In 1963 an unfortunate mixture of alcohol and pills put an early end to the life of Song Star Dinah Washington.

Cassandra Wilson. One evening, surfing the internet, I ran across a comment on a jazz music message board, it read: "When you worship at the shrine of Cassandra Wilson, she is never regarded as the 'hottest thing out there,' " the note replying to a previous message, "She is the Supreme Highness of Jazz to come sit at the feet of Billie, Sarah, Ella, and Carmen." Vocalist, arranger, and composer Cassandra Wilson deserves mention here because she is one of the heirs of those Song Stars who started with the bands. There are no Big Bands today, as we knew them, to boost her career. Rock rhythms are her background, but she deals in the other facets too. She tends to originate her repertoire, rather than follow the old stuff, and remains a Song Star of the future. However, her rendition of Billie Holiday's *I*

Wished on the Moon is the closest Cassandra Wilson comes to the Big Band Era's legacy as far as I can tell.

Lee Wiley. Hardly a jazz singer, but a genuine Song Star, Lee Wiley's personal phrasing and tone fit the musical demeanor that was Eddie Condon's 1930's and '40's band featured at his Greenwich Village, New York, nightspot. Her sophisticated style on Broadway songs moved them over into the jazz idiom. One of the most popular 1930's singers, she sang with devastating sex appeal and great instincts of what was best for her voice. A song architect, carefully designing and building until arriving in musical balance and performance, Lee's late career recording of *West of the Moon* in 1956 is an example of that special skill. William B. Williams and Jonathan Schwartz of New York's WNEW radio played Wiley frequently during the Seventies and Eighties, especially the albums of the works of George Gershwin and Cole Porter that she recorded early in her career. Her influence was notably cornetist Bix Biederbecke, whom she emulated; but Billie Holiday emulated her, as did Peggy Lee. Her last public performance was at the Newport Jazz Festival in 1972, reuniting her with Eddie Condon. She died in 1975, a legend in her time. Get a copy of *I've Got a Crush on You* recorded with Bobby Hackett's trumpet backup. Even though her early work with Max Kaminsky made her reputation, I liked her work with the Billy Butterfield RCA albums much better. Get those albums and you'll see why she is considered a great Song Star.

A special note about some others: Profiles of Song Stars **Sarah Vaughan**, **Margaret Whiting**, **The Andrews Sisters** and **Patty Andrews**, **Kay Starr**, and **Fran Warren** were profiled in the first book in this series, *The Best Damn Trumpet Player*.

My friend Patty Andrews (center) and her sisters Maxine (left) and Laverne. (Richard Grudens Collection)

**Song Stars L to R: Beryl Davis, Connie Haines and Jane Russell.
Reach out to their audience. (Connie Haines Collection)**

HONORABLE MENTIONS

Some More "Chicks"

Vera Lynn, a most revered English vocalist with the Bert Ambrose Band in London especially during World War II, who sang those stirring songs that helped win the war, *We'll Meet Again*, *The Last Time I Saw Paris*, and *They'll Be Bluebirds Over the White Cliffs of Dover*. **Beryl Davis**, remembered as the girl who sang *I'll Be Seeing You* with Glenn Miller's Air Force Band the night before he disappeared over the English Channel in 1944, who is still active in California today especially with her friends **Connie Haines** and **Jane Russell**. She has delivered the *Star Spangled Banner* 15 times at Dodgers Stadium.

    Shirley Ross who forged her first mark with the Gus Arnheim band before recording *Thanks for the Memory* with Bob Hope from the movie *The Big Broadcast of 1938*. It became Bob's famous theme. And pretty **Frances Wayne.** How about her efforts with both Charlie Barnet and Woody Herman? Her personal best: *Happiness Is a Thing Called Joe.*

    Do you remember a perky **Eydie Gorme** who first starred with trombonist Tex Beneke in the late 1940's, drumming up all those original Glenn Miller charts for the faithful? Catch her version of *If He Walked into My Life*. And there was lovely **Louise Tobin** who warbled with Will Bradley and three neat singers, **Lucy Ann Polk, Jo Ann Greer** and **Eileen Wilson,** who also graced the early Les Brown bandstand.

    It was with Paul Whiteman alumni Henry Busse's band where the **King Sisters** (Allyce, Yvonne, Donna and Louise), one of the most technically accomplished girl singing groups to emerge from the Big Band Era, initiated their career, although they later moved on to sing briefly with Horace Heidt and his Musical Knights. The girls sang for

Richard Grudens and Woody Herman talk "Song Stars" 1982. (Photo by Gus Young)

a few bands but their tenure with Alvino Rey, a former Heidt guitarist to whom Louise was married, was their most notable. Remember the *Hut-Sut Song*, *Milkman Keep Those Bottles Quiet* and The Trolley Song. They went on to appear on their own *King Family* television show in the 1960's, spawning a few albums with sales lasting into the seventies which included *Street Of Dreams* and *Don't Get Around Much Anymore*.

Del Courtney's premier vocalist was **Dotty Dotson,** performing mostly at the Claremont Hotel in Berkeley, California. **Kay Weber's** duration with Bob Crosby's group was short but musically effective. Don't forget sexy **Abbe Lane** who kept the Rumba King Xavier Cugat's band popular with her dynamic vocals.

Lillian Clark Oliver, one of the original Ray Charles Singers and once a Pied Piper, appeared on the Perry Como Show in the '50's and recorded with Count Basie, Tommy Dorsey, Louis Armstrong, the Norman Luboff Choir and the Ray Coniff singers. What a career! **Peg LaCentra,** Artie Shaw's first singer ever, dubbed the singing voices of actresses Ida Lupino and Susan Hayward. She also sang with Benny Goodman, and in 1939 she starred in *The Peg LaCentra Show* for NBC radio. Lest we forget, the **Ray Charles Singers** has featured many lady Song Stars over the years.

Edythe Wright sang some smoothies with Tommy Dorsey just before the Sinatra/Haines/Pied Pipers era. Eddy Duchin featured the **DeMarco Sisters** high atop the Waldorf-Astoria for a while before their prolific engagements in Las Vegas. And speaking of sisters, there were the **DeCastro Sisters, Babette, Cherie, and Peggy,** who emigrated from the Dominican Republic, a close-harmony trio who was extremely popular in the '50's, selling millions of copies of *Teach Me Tonight*. One of my favorite people ever, **Marie Ellington**, devoted wife of Nat "King" Cole and mother of Natalie Cole, sang beautifully with the Duke during the band's heyday. And further thanks to her for endorsing our first book, *The Best Damn Trumpet Player*.

British born **Mabel Mercer**, her mother a music hall performer, was first a dancer. She sang those out-of-the-way type songs in a subdued manner usually only with a piano and mostly in small clubs. A singer's singer, **Mabel** influenced folks like Frank Sinatra, Lena Horne, and Nat "King" Cole, by their own admissions.

Future movie stars **June Haver** and **Betty Grable** got their start with Ted Fio Rito in the mid-Thirties. Betty made some sides with husband Harry James too. Do you remember **Eugenie Baird's** vocals with Glen Gray and his Casa Loma Orchestra? Lovely **Ruth Robin** graced the Phil Harris bandstand in the Thirties with her rhythmic phrasings. **June Hutton** was the popular girl singer with Ina Ray Hutton's blonde bombshell, all-girl band in the late Thirties. June also became a Pied Piper after Jo Stafford left the group and was on the recording of *Dream*. The **Skylarks** made a melodic difference with Harry James' band while he worked in the movies.

Broadway star **Vivian Blaine's** first efforts animated Al Kavelin's New York City band in the Thirties by singing *Love Is Gone*, and **Dorothy Lamour** began it all in Herbie Kay's band in 1934 singing at the Blackhawk Restaurant in Chicago before all those Hope/Crosby flicks. **Ann Richards** was a latter star of the Stan Kenton band in the late Forties. The **Barrie Sisters** were the "Waltz King" Wayne King's magical vocalists in the thirties. Among many others, **Dolores Hawkins** and **Ginnie Powell** took turns vocalizing with the Gene Krupa and Boyd Raeburn bands.

Prolific maestro Kay Kyser and his "Kollege of Musical Knowledge" headlined **Ginny Sims** and **Georgia Carroll. Ginny's** CD release entitled *There Goes That Song Again* is a worthwhile tribute to this worthy Big Band Song Star. Guy Lombardo featured his sister **Rosemarie Lombardo** on the vocals, and Johnny Long sponsored **Julie Wilson** as his very fine girl singer. Benny also starred **Lisa Morrow** singing *Give Me the Simple Life*—so good, too!

Bouncy movie star **Betty Hutton** first sang with Vincent Lopez in New York and her sister **Marion Hutton** was a star with Glenn Miller in the Forties. I love her swinging version of *Ding, Dong, the Witch Is Dead*. **Marion** joined Miller in 1938, and, except for a brief period in 1941 when she took time off to have a baby, she remained until September 1942. **Dorothy Claire** filled in for **Marion** during that period. Song stylist **Mindy Carson's** refrains started with Johnny Messner expressing the band's theme *Can't We Be Friends* before she went off on her own. **Pat Collins'** fine efforts with my old friend Moe Zudecoff (you know him as Buddy Morrow) and his original band, before he fronted Tommy Dorsey's ghost band, were first rate. Of

Kay Kyser's Ginny Sims 1941.
(Richard Grudens Collection)

Marion Hutton with Glenn Miller in 1940. (Jack Ellsworth Collection)

course, **Harriet Hilliard** was bandleader Ozzie Nelson's swinging vocalist, future wife, radio/tv partner, and, later, mother of lightweight rock and roller legendary Ricky Nelson.

Besides Dinah Shore and Lee Wiley, **Anita Boyer** also contributed to Leo Reisman's Boston orchestra. Anita was also with Tommy D. Bandleader Buddy Rogers (married later to movie star Mary Pickford) showcased **Marilyn Maxwell** (known then as **Marvel Maxwell**) in the late Twenties in New York City.

Movie beauty and Connie Haines' singing buddy **Jane Russell** took her turn band singing with Kay Kyser as did **Toni Arden** with Al Trace. **Carolyn Grey**, a Peggy Lee-like singer sang with Gene Krupa and Woody Herman. Check out her Boogie Blues..."scats" and all. Blues belter **Vicky Lee** did it all on *Baby Don't Love Me No More* with Lionel Hampton.

Nan Wynn did the honors with Raymond Scott, as did his wife-to-be **Dorothy Collins,** especially with the radio and television shows *Your Hit Parade*. Artie Shaw established many Song Stars in his band including **Anita Bradley, Bonnie Lake,** and **Georgia Gibbs. Ella Mae Morse's** wonderful, classic rendition of *Cow, Cow, Boogie* shored up the Freddie Slack Band for a long while. Song stylist **Jane Morgan** did some time with Dick Stabile and his band before her solo career took off. You will remember her version of *Fascination*. **June Richmond** was with Cab Calloway on *Angels with Dirty Eyes* and with Jimmy Dorsey too.

Besides our Song Star **Kitty Kallen**, the Jack Teagarden orchestra supported vocalists **Linda Keene, Phyllis Lane** and **Sally Lang**, as well as **Jean Arnold.** Song Star **Fran Warren,** featured in *The Best Damn Trumpet Player* book, shared the "mike" with **Jane Essex, Kay Doyle, Lillian Lane** and **Maxine Sullivan** in the band of Claude Thornhill.

Bandleader Orrin Tucker told me not too long ago that he discovered **Bonnie Baker** and was convinced she could be a singing star. "I brought her into the band and, early in 1939, while we were playing in the Cocoanut Grove in Los Angeles, we recorded *Oh Johnny* for Columbia. In a few months she was one of the hottest singers in the nation, making our band a big national attraction." **Bonnie** almost eclipsed the name of Orrin Tucker. He never would feature a singer

205

after that experience. Tommy Tucker's band showcased **Amy Arnell** in his 1930's appearances mostly in the midwest. Film singer **Alice Faye** articulated her early efforts with Rudy Vallee's band in the Thirties, and Fred Waring and his Pennsylvanians featured the voices of the harmonious **Lane Sisters (Rosemary, Priscilla, and Lola)**. Speaking of sister groups, hats off to the still performing **McGuire Sisters, Phyllis, Christine, and Dorothy,** especially for *May You Always* and *Sincerely* and to the **Chordettes** for *Mr. Sandman* recorded with Archie Bleyer. Surprise for most girl singer fans: The Anson Weeks orchestra highlighted none other than **Dale Evans**, future wife of the "King of the Cowboys" himself, Roy Rogers. She was a soulful singer. **Kay St.Germaine** and **June Knight** also participated in Weeks' group as did Tony Martin and Bob Crosby. Kay became the featured singer with Eddie Cantor on his radio show. Besides the Lennon Sisters, **Alice Lon, Lois Best** and **Jo Ann Hubbard**, as well as **Roberta Lynn,** also articulated their melodies throughout the years with bandleader Lawrence Welk And a mention for **Daryl Sherman** who has played piano with Dick Sudhalter's band and many all-star sidemen, including people like bassist Jay Leonhart. I interviewed her in the late Eighties and she was a definite, upcoming Song Star then.

June Valli started with *Godfrey's Talent Scouts* and performed with the bands of both Ralph Flanagan and Art Mooney. June was a summer replacement for Andy Williams and worked with Johnny Carson and my pal Bob Hope. She was the voice of "Chiquita Banana." **Peggy Clark (one of the Clark Sisters)** from North Dakota sang during the war at USO spots and then with Tommy Dorsey from 1943 to 1945. She also sang with the **Skylarks** in the Harry James band. **Sue Allen Brown** warbled with Benny Goodman and the *Hit Parade* orchestras and recorded with Henry Mancini, Mel Torme' and Les Baxter. As the renamed **Sentimentalists**, the **Clark Sisters** big hit was *Sunny Side of the Street* with Tommy Dorsey.

Helen Grayco worked with both the Spike Jones Band and Stan Kenton (at the Hollywood Palladium). She married Spike Jones. *Love and Marriage* and *Teach Me Tonight* were her best hits with RCA. It was **Mary Ann McCall** who sang with Tommy Dorsey in 1938, Woody Herman in 1939, and Charlie Barnet in 1940. She was a great jazz singer admired by jazzmen. **Gloria Wood** was a singer with

Horace Heidt, Hal McIntyre, and Kay Kyser. She was one of the Johnny Mann Singers and had a great hit with the *Woody Woodpecker Song*. **Virginia Craig Pruett** was also a revered Song Star who sang with Bob Crosby, Billy May, Wilbur Hatch and with the Hilo's, one of the best singing groups ever. And true Song Star **Gilda Maiken (Anderson)**, one of the famous Skylarks and founders of the Society of Singers, was a sensation on the Dinah Shore TV shows for years and sang with the bands of Herman, J. Dorsey, and James. **Paula Kelly** was wonderful too, best remembered for her membership in the Modernaires singing group with Glenn Miller, although she started with Dick Stabile and later sang with Artie Shaw. **Ginny Mancini**, wife of the wonderful Henry Mancini, sang with Tex Beneke's band after the war, "...an experience I treasure," says Ginny. **Jeanne Hazard**, nee **Taylor** began with Jimmy Greer and Jan Savitt and recorded with Count Basie. Forget not **Lil Armstrong** who sang with husband Satchmo, but also ran her own band in 1937. Catch her *Bluer Than Blue*.

Irene Day was a Krupa Song Star and then joined Charlie Spivak whom she eventually married. And remember that bandleader beautiful **Ina Ray Hutton** who also sang pretty good with her own band.

Harry James also featured **Gail Robbins**. Her interpretation of Gershwin's *I've Got a Crush on You* is just elegant. **Della Reese**, current TV angel, did it well with Erskine Hawkins in the early '50's. And, how could you forget **Dorothy Dandridge's** rendition of *Chattanooga Choo-Choo* in the film *Sun Valley Serenade* with Glenn.

A special mention for **Kathryn Crosby**, a Song Star in her own right these days appearing recently on Broadway in *State Fair*. Even though she never sang with the bands, she certainly spent a lot of time singing with someone else we know who did. Kathryn's alto may not be a classic, but, as she acknowledged to me, "......there's still time."

Any one of these Song Stars could make or break a band. Their joyful voices, filling the air with melodic expression backed by a multitude of talented musicians, prolific arrangers, and innovative band leaders, furnished us with the musical nutrition we needed when we needed it most.

For one reason or another some of these vocalists exited the business almost as quickly as they entered leaving their personal, indelible mark upon the musical landscape. Leave it to say these Song Stars punctuated the Big Band Era by providing us with some first-rate versions of this century's best composed melodies. The memory of their works will remain with us until we draw our own last breath.

It may just be the recollection of a single song at a very special moment in our lifetime. How much do we owe The Song Stars for that alone? How can we repay them for such a personal gift? Some things don't carry a price tag.

I hope I haven't omitted any one.

THE SOCIETY OF SINGERS

Credo:
It's Time The Rare Bird Called A Singer
Had Some Tender Loving Care.

Their membership roster lists almost every known living entertainer. The Chairman of the Board is none other than Frank Sinatra. Ginny Mancini is the President. Burt Bacharach is a member, as is Pat Boone, Steve Allen, and Les Brown. So is Liz Smith, Peter Yarrow, Michael Feinstein, Quincy Jones, and Perry Como. Bea Wain is Secretary. Composer Jay Livingston is on the Board of Directors; Keely Smith sits on the Advisory Council; and Bob and Dolores Hope are top contributors as well as members.

What about this organization? What does it do and why?

Some time ago the Society membership chairman, Ray Charles (known as the *other* Ray Charles-leader of that famous choir), published a letter prefaced in an effort to solicit new members and inquired accordingly:

> If you've ever ENJOYED a singer—
> If you've ever EMPLOYED a singer—
> If you've ever EXPLOITED a singer—

then join the Society of Singers.

The premise contends that, although many singers and other performers who produced hit records during the Big Band Era and beyond achieved lasting fame, they didn't necessarily achieve lasting fortune. Being one of the exploiters, a writer about singers, I was happy to join.

The Society cites the case of Bob Eberly, the prolific singer who recorded hit after hit with Jimmy Dorsey (*Green Eyes*, *Amapola*,

Besame Mucho, Marie Elena, I Understand). He was paid about thirty-five dollars for each of those recording dates. The songs sold millions, but he never received a dime in royalties. That was the arrangement, as many others who suffered the same fate will testify. I remember Patty Andrews telling me that all three Andrews Sisters received a total of $50.00 for recording *Bie Mir Bist Du Shoen.* Fran Warren also told me that's exactly what she received for her hit recording of *Sunday Kind Of Love* with Claude Thornhill. That's the way it was in those days, and it was true up unto the last decade or so. The songwriters and publishers collected every time a song was played on the radio or TV—but the singer didn't collect a dime.

Hence, the Society of Singers.

It is well-known that Frank Sinatra footed the bill when Bob Eberly became ill and passed away. But Frank, no matter how much money he was willing to donate for such worthy charity, even though he only knew Eberly slightly, could not possibly continue such generosity on his own.

Hence, The Society of Singers.

And, as the letter continued, "when Flo Ballard of the Supremes died on welfare, it wasn't because she'd blown a fortune. The record company made the fortune, not the Supremes."

Thus, the Society of Singers, whose goal in the short term is to build a fund to help singers who require medical or any kind of emergency care, assisting singers in need on a strictly confidential basis. In the long term, it hopes to provide a retirement home and other pertinent facilities.

It all began with an idea by then President Gilda Maiken Anderson and Secretary Donna Manners in the early Eighties and was known as The Singers Aid Foundation. A corporate resolution renamed it The Society Of Singers, a non-profit entity, in 1985. Charter Members were Gilda Maiken Anderson (former band singer), Ginny Mancini (former band singer, wife of Henry Mancini), Tony Martin (the one and only), Tess Russell, Randy Van Horne, Donna Manners, and Anthony Adams.

Early members prolific producer Budd Granoff and his wife Kitty Kallen were instrumental in raising the initially needed funds when the Society first formed, by producing an album entitled *A Gift Of*

Music which was a financial success. Kitty told me she is so proud of that.

Since then the Society has networked with other active relief funds to provide maximum financial benefits for deserving applicants. Each Society newsletter abounds with "thank you" letters from recipients of this most welcome assistance.

The Society holds many benefits, and members willingly and happily show up in abundance to perform. Recently, a gala benefit, *The Ladies Who Sang with the Bands,* was held in Los Angeles. Everyone was there: Gogi Grant, Bea Wain, Carol Burnett, Helen Forrest, Kay Starr, Fran Warren, Anita O'Day, The King Sisters, Beryl Davis, Connie Haines, and Bea Arthur....to name a few. Lee Hale, Society director and prolific veteran musical producer, and Ray Charles produced the show. Lee sent me a two-hour video of the entire show. It was wonderful. They had a remarkable time and the Society raised a few more bucks to pay back rent or finance a medical proceedure for a down-and-out singer somewhere in our great United States.

When Ella Fitzgerald died, the family members requested that any memorial contributions be made to the Society. Ella's heart was always with the Society of Singers.

Once a year the Society bestows an "Ella Fitzgerald Lifetime Achievement Award" called an "Ella" on a deserving singer. In 1994, it was awarded to Peggy Lee. In 1995, it was presented to Steve Lawrence and Eydie Gorme'. In the Summer of 1997 Lena Horne will be honored at Avery Fisher Hall at Lincoln Center, New York, in an all-star salute on the occasion of her eightieth birthday.

Come, join with them; they'd love to have you. Contact the Society at 8242 West 3rd Street, Suite 250, Los Angeles, California 90048 or at (213) 651-1696. And tell membership chairman Ray Charles that I sent you. He'll be happy to sign you up.

Song Stars Bibliography

The Hornes, Gail Lumet Buckley, Alfred A. Knopf, 1986

The Swing Era, Gunther Schuller, Oxford University Press, 1989

Jazz Singing, Will Friedwald, Macmillan Publishing Co., New York 1990-92

The Big Bands, George Simon, Macmillan Publishing Co., New York 1967

Big Band Almanac, Leo Walker, Vinewood Enterprises, Hollywood, Ca. 1978

The Encyclopedia of Jazz, Leonard Feather & Ira Gitler, Horizon Press, New York 1976

That Lucky Old Son, Frankie Laine and Joseph F. Laredo, Pathfinder Publishing,Ventura,Ca. 1993

A Pictorial History of Radio, Irving Settel, Castle Books, Secaucus, New Jersey 1970

The Great American Popular Singers, Henry Pleasants, Simon and Schuster, New York 1974

Doris Day, Her Own Story, A. E. Hotchner, William Morrow, New York 1975

The Complete Entertainment Discography, Brian Rust, Arlington House, New Rochelle, NY 1973

Josephine, Josephine Baker and Jo Bouillon, Harper & Row, New York 1976

Call Me Lucky, Bing Crosby with Pete Martin, Simon and Schuster, New York 1953

This for Remembrance, Rosemary Clooney & Raymond Strait, Playboy Press, New York 1977

For Once in My Life, Connie Haines and Robert B. Stone, Connie Haines Publishing, Clearwater Beach, Fla. 1976

Dick Haymes Society Newsletters, compiled by Maurice Dunn and Roger Dooner, Birmingham, England & Minneapois, Minnesota Various dates

Big Band Jump Newsletters, Hagen Williams, Don Kennedy, Atlanta, Georgia. Various dates

TV Guide, The First 25 Years, Edited by Jay S. Harris, Simon and Schuster, NY 1978

The Last Christmas Show, Bob Hope and Pete Martin, Doubleday & Co., New York 1974

The Cotton Club, Jim Haskins, Hippocrene Books, New York 1977

All You Need is Love, The Story of Popular Music, Tony Palmer, Grossman Publishers, New York 1976

Music is My Mistress, Edward Kennedy Ellington, Doubleday & Co., New York 1973

Singers and the Song, Gene Lees, Oxford University Press, New York 1987

WNEW, Where the Melody Lingers On, Nightingale Gordon, New York 1984

Bing Crosby, A Bio-Bibliography, J. Roger Osterholm Greenwood Press, Westport, Conn. 1994

Index

216

217

218

219

220

Redman, Don, 181
Reed, Rex, 149, 170
Reese, Della, 10, 207
Reisman, Leo, 189, 205
Rey, Alvino, 201
Rhythm Boys, 30
Rich, Buddy, 10, 20
Rich, Freddy, 9
Richards, Ann, 134, 202
Richmond, June, 205
Riddle, Nelson, 74, 91, 99, 100
Rinker, Al , 30
Roach, Max, 186
Robeson, 41, 111, 115
Robin, Ruth, 202
Robbins, Gail, 8, 207
Roberts, Lynn, 8, 20, 163-171
Robinson, Bill"Bojangles", 117, 119
Rodgers & Hart, 37, 91, 92, 156
Rogers, Buddy, 205
Rogers, Ginger, 73, 124
Rogers, Roy, 103, 206
Rollins, Sonny, 182
Romano, Tony, 125-127
Rooney, Mickey, 67
Ross, Jerry, 98
Ross, Shirley, 199
Rowland, Helen, 9
Rowles, Jimmy, 176
Rushing, Jimmy, 185
Russell, Jane, 69-70, 198-199, 205
Russell, Tess, 210
Ruth, Babe, 113

Sachs, Mannie, 75
Safranski, Eddie, 184
Sanders, Felicia, 10
Saroyan, William, 98
Sauter, Eddie, 46
Savitt, Jan, 55, 207
Schuller, Gunther, 57
Schuur, Diane, 10
Schwab, Laurence, 113
Schwartz, Jonathan, 36, 196
Scott, Hazel, 115
Scott, Raymond, 134, 205
Sentimentalists, The, 206

Severinson, Doc, 170
Shaw, Arnold, 153
Shaw, Artie, 4, 6, 8, 45-46, 55, 59, 84,
    96, 115, 154, 174, 201, 205, 207
Shearing, George, 13, 15, 142
Sherman, Daryl, 206
Shore, Dinah, 4, 10, 17, 98, 134, 154,
    188-189, 205, 207
Short, Bobby, 36
Shribman, Joe, 98
Signoret, Simone, 120
Silvers, Phil, 127
Simon, George, 29, 97
Simon, Paul , 37
Simone, Nina, 174
Sims, Ginny, 6, 202-203
Sims, Sylvia, 10
Sinatra, Frank, 10, 19-20, 29-30, 37, 48,
    51, 58, 60-61, 64-66, 78, 90-93, 119,
    -120, 124, 132, 154, 167, 169, 189,
    201, 209-210
Sinatra, Frank Jr., 49
Sissle, Noble, 8, 41, 110, 114, 181
Skylarks, The, 202, 206-207
Slack, Freddie, 205
Sloane, Carol, 10
Smith, Bessie, 22-25, 27, 30, 37, 105,
    193, 195
Smith, C.Camille, 158, 160
Smith, Carrie, 9
Smith, Cliff, 84
Smith, Kate, 37, 66, 153, 191
Smith, Keely, 4, 10, 17, 128, 169, 189-
    190, 209
Smith, Liz, 209
Snyder, Jeanette, 151
Society of Singers, 4, 60, 86, 93, 142,
    190-191, 206-207, 209-211
Somers, Joannie, 9
Southern, Jerri, 10
Sperling, Jack, 135
Spivak, Charlie, 165, 174, 195, 207
Stabile, Dick, 205, 207
Stafford, Jo, 2, 6, 19, 20, 49, 58, 65, 93,
    103, 128, 130-136, 151, 169, 202
Stafford Sisters, 131

222